A STONE OF HOPE

To Elizabeth

Johny B, Thom

2-9-2018

Glendora MS.

A STONE OF HOPE

*Rising Above Slavery, Jim Crow,
and Poverty in Glendora, Mississippi*

JOHNNY B. THOMAS / THOMAS J. DURANT, JR.

A Publishing Management & Consulting Company

Rev. date: 11/15/2017

CONTENTS

Dedication vii

Acknowledgments ix

Foreword xi

Preface xiii

Chapter 1   A Stone of Hope: Introduction 1

Chapter 2   A History of Glendora 5

Chapter 3   The Burden of Slavery 12

Chapter 4   Let My People Go 17

Chapter 5   The Black Codes and Jim Crow 22

Chapter 6   Sharecropping: A New Form of Slavery 26

Chapter 7   The Johnny B. Thomas Story 31

Chapter 8   Matriarchs and Patriarchs 50

Chapter 9   The Emmett Till Memorial Commission 108

Chapter 10   The Community Revitalization Movement 115

Chapter 11   Cultural Heritage Tourism 119

Chapter 12   Building The Emmett Till Historic Intrepid Center ... 127

Chapter 13   Grand Tour of The The Emmett Till Museum 134

Chapter 14   Mother Mamie Mobley
             and Women in The Civil Rights Movement 160

Chapter 15   Unresolved Civil Rights Murders 165

Chapter 16   The Emmett Till Heritage Trail 169

Epilogue 175

Dedication

WE DEDICATE THIS book to the late Mrs. Shirley T. Thomas, first lady of the town of Glendora, whose persistent efforts helped to advance equality for all residents of Glendora, especially the youth, and for fighting for fair treatment in the workplace against all forms of employment discrimination in Tallahatchie County, where there is a long history of discrimination against blacks in the workplace. Her spirit continues to inspire others to continue the fight for equality, social justice, and civil rights. I express abiding thanks to my mother, Adeline Hill, who somehow cared for her eight children as a single parent and to my father, Mr. Henry Lee Loggins, who did all he could to help our family survive after being forced to abandon his family as a result of the Emmett Till kidnapping and brutal lynching. I give thanks to the citizens of the community of Glendora for allowing me to share my vision for the community over the past 30 years and for working for the future of our youth. Finally, I would like to thank my children, Miss Loretta Mcgee, Mr. Tyrus Davis, Miss Pamela Williams, Mr. Prentiss Williams, Miss Marsheka Smith, the late Mr. Leslie D. Johnson, and my grandchildren and great grandchildren.

Acknowledgments

W E ACKNOWLEDGE THE following individuals for their contributions to the completion of this book: To my late wife, Shirley T. Thomas, for her patience with me as Mayor for more than 13 years; Dr. Thomas James Durant, Jr., for discovering and assisting me and the community in telling our story; Dr. Neari F. Warner, for meticulously editing the entire manuscript; Mrs. Florida B. Smith, Mrs. Beatrice Smith, Mrs. Christine V. Wheeler, Mr. Curtis L. Anderson, Mr. James Madyun, and Mr. Eddie Meeks, for their interviews; Miss Temita Davis, for the photos used on the book's cover; Ms. Angelic Willingham, for designing the cover of the book; Michael Verrett, for work on the book's cover; Mr. Simeon Wright and his wife Annie Wright, Rev. and Mrs. Wheeler Parker, and other family members, for the information provided on the Emmett Till story; Miss Temita Davis and Dr. Marvin Haire, consultants in the development of the ETHIC Museum; Mr. Al White, consultant for the audio and video development for the ETHIC Museum; Mr. Bobby Rush, for his interviews used in the development of the Sonny Boy Williamson Bed and Breakfast; The Honorable Bennie G. Thompson, Congressman for the 2nd District of Mississippi, for writing the Foreword and helping to secure funding for the community development projects in Glendora; and the Mamie Till Mobley Memorial Foundation, Mrs. Arica Gordon Taylor, Executive Director, and Mrs. Ollie Gordon, for allowing the town of Glendora to host the seventieth birthday of Emmett Louis Till. We also would like to thank all of the matriarchs, patriarchs, and residents, who fought for civil rights and against civil wrongs in Glendora and Tallahatchie County, Mississippi.

Foreword

UNDERSTANDING THE HISTORY of Glendora, Mississippi helps one to appreciate why this story must be told. The events surrounding the murder of a fourteen-year-old Black boy in the Deep South during a time of rapid social change is significant. Indeed, it was a seminal event for many in Mississippi and throughout the Nation. Serving as Congressman for the Second Congressional District of Mississippi since 1993 has reinforced my belief that "fighting the good fight" begins with being rooted in our history.

This book is of personal importance to me because of my decades-long relationship with the author, Johnny B. Thomas. We have worked side-by-side to build up our communities and to make a better Mississippi. Johnny and I share many similarities in the strides we have taken in serving our communities and thrusting ourselves into the political environment of rural Mississippi towns and beyond. We have shared experiences as alderman, mayors and county supervisors. Not only have we shared some of the same positions, but we share a similar world view that is reflective of our goal to continue to advocate on behalf of the voiceless.

This book is a true reflection of the trials, tribulations, and triumphs of Glendora, Mississippi. It serves as a literary guide through the rich history of Glendora and the oppressed south. It tells the story of the establishment of the institution of slavery and the disparity of the Jim Crow South. It immerses into the tragic death of Emmett Till and details the effects the Civil Rights Movement had on rural

Mississippi. The book also highlights the importance of political involvement in the African-American community through Johnny's own personal story. The experiences and historical narratives that will be taken from reading this book demonstrate the importance of looking back at our history in order to move forward.

Mr. Thomas is a pillar of his community and has served the people of Glendora, Mississippi for over 35 years. There is no better person to tell this story than one who has successfully overcome many trials and tribulations before triumphantly becoming a *Stone of Hope* in Glendora, Mississippi.

Congressman Bennie G. Thompson
Second Congressional District of Mississippi

Preface

THIS BOOK IS about the past, present, and future of Glendora, a small town located in the heart of the Mississippi Delta. The story begins with the history of Glendora, including slavery, which was the root of many evils that plagued the people of this small rural town for several centuries. In this book, we reveal the historical influences of slavery and Jim Crow on the social and economic status of multi-generations of families of Glendora. We provide firsthand experiences and eyewitness accounts of the harshness of the living conditions of sharecroppers who worked on local plantations, the prevalence of rural poverty and its effects on the lives of the residents, and how all of these conditions created a "mountain of despair" for the people of Glendora.

This book provides vivid details of the brutal and tragic murder of Emmett Till and the trial of the offenders that left a legacy of violence and injustices that energized the Civil Rights Movement in America. However, the story of Glendora is about more than the murder of Emmett Till. It is also about the influence of this tragedy on the lives of the people of Glendora and the surrounding area of Tallahatchie County. While many books and films have dealt with the role of the Emmett Till murder in the civil and human rights movement, little attention has been given to the lives of the people who live in the communities where the tragedy occurred, and how they have overcome many civil and human wrongs that were inflicted upon many generations of people. A variety of firsthand observations and experiences of matriarchs and patriarchs of Glendora and Tallahatchie are used to provide a reconstructed view of lives of sharecroppers, as well as historical knowledge and intriguing facts surrounding the untold story and continuing saga of the Emmett Till murder and trial.

This book also deals with the resilience of the people of Glendora in attempting to transform their "mountain of despair" into a "stone of hope" that Dr. Martin Luther King, Jr. referred to in his "I Have A Dream" speech in Washington, D.C. in August 1963. With great faith and determination, and the leadership of Mayor Johnny B. Thomas, the residents of Glendora decided to pursue a course of civic engagement to create the Emmett Till Historic Intrepid Center and to promote education and awareness about civil rights, and to promote cultural heritage tourism for community development and revitalization. Through much hard work and determination, many of the crooked places have been made straight and rough places have been made smooth; however, Glendora is continuing its struggle for full transformation into that "stone of hope" that Dr. King envisioned.

CHAPTER 1
A STONE OF HOPE: INTRODUCTION

D R. MARTIN LUTHER King, Jr. spoke these words in his famous "I Have A Dream" speech in Washington, D.C. on August 28, 1963, which re-energized the Civil Rights Movement in America:

> I have a dream that one day every valley shall be exalted, every hill and mountain shall be made low. The rough places will be made plain, and the crooked places will be made straight. And the glory of the Lord shall be revealed, and all flesh shall see it together. This is our hope. This is the faith that I go back to the South with. With this faith, we will be able to hew out of a mountain of despair a stone of hope.

Glendora, Mississippi was one of those "rough places" in the South with a history that epitomized a "mountain of despair." The ancestors of its African American residents were in bondage that endured for more than a century, followed by a new form of slavery called sharecropping. The history of Glendora also included forced exploitation of black laborers that created widespread poverty, and Jim Crow laws and customs that resulted in widespread violence

JOHNNY B. THOMAS / THOMAS J. DURANT, JR.

in the form of murders, lynches, rapes, beatings, incarceration, and destruction of families that were common in Glendora and Tallahatchie County, Mississippi and throughout the South, during both the antebellum and postbellum periods. During the Jim Crow era, at least a dozen lynchings were reported in Tallahatchie County, including two blacks who were hanged in Glendora in 1906. In the wake of plantation servitude and sharecropping, Glendora and the surrounding areas in the Mississippi Delta became one of the most economically depressed regions in the country. Dr. King was right when he referred to the "mountain of despair" because this was the condition that plagued Glendora and other black communities in the American South for more than a century.

Another significant event that contributed to the "mountain of despair" in Glendora, occurred in 1955, when a 14-year-old boy named Emmett Till was brutally murdered by two white men. This horrific murder of a black child left a tragic legacy in Glendora and Tallahatchie County. The Emmett Till murder ignited the Civil Rights Movement in Glendora, Tallahatchie County, Mississippi, the South, and the nation and caused an explosion of racial conflict and strife. The Emmett Till murder also left deep physical and emotional pains and scars that affected both black and white families in the Glendora area. Although the Emmett Till murder is well-known by many, a countless number of murders of black people, known and unknown, was committed by whites throughout the South during the Post-Emancipation period and the Civil Rights Era.

The town of Glendora is still haunted by lingering mysteries surrounding the "untold story" of the murder of Emmett Till. While people are still appalled by the Emmett Till murder, journalistic news reports, and commentaries have given only cursory attention to the social and cultural conditions of the people and communities that surrounded the Emmett Till murder and trial, and have underestimated the burden that this tragedy placed on Glendora and other communities and how it hampered their capacity to rise above their past circumstances. Many people have asked whether or not Glendora can become known for more than the town where Emmett Till was murdered? And can it overcome past tragic circumstances, including widespread impoverishment, created and perpetuated by the neo-slavery system of sharecropping, subsistence agriculture, and Jim Crow laws and customs?

The Emmett Till murder also helped to accelerate the decline of sharecropping, plantation agriculture, and the perceived image of the "idyllic" southern life as it was known in the South. Seeking to escape the effusive injustices and resentment that evolved from the tragic Emmett Till murder, many blacks migrated from Mississippi and other southern states in search of better opportunities and a better life in Memphis, Chicago, Detroit, St. Louis, and other cities in the North, Mid-West, and West. This outmigration included many of the people from the town of Glendora and Tallahatchie County. Consequently, at different intervals in Glendora, the cotton gin closed, banks and other businesses closed, and the Amtrak train depot closed. In addition, the grueling struggle for civil rights and the elimination of racial discrimination and inequality that occurred between 1960 and 1970, led to white flight from the area that left the town of Glendora mostly "black and poor." Whites sold or abandoned their houses or businesses and fled the town in droves, taking mostly all of the economic resources with them. In the aftermath of the Civil Rights Movement, the educational system began to deteriorate, and Glendora was plagued by insufficient economic resources for the development and maintenance of public services and facilities for its residents. Almost overnight, Glendora became a "ghost town" with a high rate of poverty among the families and residents, who have been referred to as the "people left behind."

This book tells a story about the trials, tribulations, and triumphs of the people of Glendora in their efforts to remove their "mountain of despair," created by past conditions, and their struggle to become a stone of hope and beacon of light to guide its people out of the darkness into the marvelous light of freedom, justice, and prosperity. A major part of the story of Glendora deals with the odyssey of Johnny B. Thomas and how he rose from the son of sharecroppers to become the Mayor of Glendora, a position he has held for the past 35 years. This book also deals with the lifelong efforts of Mayor Thomas and the people of Glendora to achieve community revitalization and economic development, including the movement to build the Emmett Till Historic Intrepid Center to promote cultural heritage tourism.

In their efforts to build the Emmett Till Historic Intrepid Center, Mayor Thomas and the residents of Glendora faced many challenges and questions. Would tourists come to Glendora to see a museum built around the tragic murder of Emmett Till in a small, isolated, rural town plagued by widespread poverty, located in the heart of the Mississippi Delta? Could the Emmett Till Historic Intrepid Center create a sufficient amount of tourism to stimulate and sustain economic development of the town? Although cultural heritage tourism had been used to facilitate economic develop in other towns, would it work in Glendora? And could the Emmett Till Historic Intrepid Center serve as a major impetus for the transformation of Glendora from "a mountain of despair" to a "stone of hope" that Dr. King referred to in his "I Have A Dream" speech in Washington, D.C. in 1963? While it was obvious that Glendora still had a long way to go, the residents found some solace in an old African American adage that says, "We ain't where we ought to be, and we ain't where we want to be, but thank God Almighty, we ain't where we used to be."

CHAPTER 2

A HISTORY OF GLENDORA

G LENDORA, MISSISSIPPI IS known as "a place where good friendships go way back and way deep" (Pat and Mike Didlake). But you can ask anyone in the area and they will tell you that Glendora has had its share of trials, tribulations and triumphs. However, in order to gain a full appreciation and understanding of the town and surrounding county, one must have knowledge of its history, including the good and bad things that made Glendora what it is today. This brief history of Glendora hopes to achieve this end.

Long before European explorers came to America, the land where Glendora is presently located was occupied by the Choctaw Tribe. The Natchez and Chickasaw Tribes also lived in the area. To this day, many of the people, places, and landmarks, including towns, lakes, creeks, rivers, and roads, bear the names of these Native American tribes. Tallahatchie, the county in which Glendora is located, is a Choctaw name that means "rock of waters." Spanish settlers and explorers arrived in the area around 1540, followed by the French, who established the first permanent European settlement in Mississippi in 1699. After the Territory of Mississippi was formed in 1798, the Choctaw and other Native Americans were pushed out of their native land into isolated and less productive areas by ruthless white settlers, who were backed by military power. Consequently,

Native Americans lost most of their land due to war, conquest, and invasions by Europeans that contributed to their demise.

The State of Mississippi, named after the Great Mississippi River that forms its western border, was added to the Union in 1817 and became the 20th state of the American Republic. The Choctaw were forced by the General Assembly of the State of Mississippi to accept a "treaty" called the "Treaty of Dancing Rabbit Creek," on September 30, 1830 (part of the infamous "Great Removal" or "Trail of Tears"). According to the treaty, the Choctaw were essentially given two options: to live on tracts of land (reservations) stipulated in the treaty, under Choctaw laws and customs; or live on land ceded to the Europeans under the laws of the United States Government. Based on the treaty, the Choctaw nation would be required to cede to the United States, the entire territory they owned and possessed, east of the Mississippi River, and move their homes and families west of the Mississippi River. As European Americans gained more and more land they gradually became the dominant culture in the State of Mississippi and the region. The Choctaw who remained on land east of the Mississippi were included in the "colored" population, which subjected them to racial segregation and exclusion practiced by the Mississippi Black Codes. During Reconstruction (1865-1877), the health, education, and economic conditions of the Choctaw were largely ignored by the Mississippi and American governments. While the Civil War was being fought, the Choctaw struggled to survive.

During the post-colonial period, Glendora was eventually established as a settlement and then as a town by European settlers. Glendora was "founded" in 1833 by European settlers who crossed the Mississippi River and followed small Indian trails into the interior of Mississippi. Settlers from Webb and other small villages in the area transported logs down the river where they were processed into lumber. These workers and their families began a settlement a short distance away near Black Bayou, which forms the southern border of present-day Glendora. As the population of the town increased, a railway was built in 1883, and a post office and a voting precinct were established to service the population. On March 19, 1900, a charter was signed by William Gay, who became the first mayor of Glendora. The town began with 83 residents. The first African American organized society, named the Benevolent Aid and Burial Society, was established in 1910, ten years after the town was incorporated, which eventually developed chapters in every county of the State of Mississippi. The family names of the African American men who formed the Society were Hawkins, Chatman, Sanders, Baskins, Thomas, Spater, Whitaker, Tyler, Lee, Hilson, Melton, and Walker. These brave men, aided by their families, formed the Benevolent Aid and Burial Society, in spite of the fact that two black men from the community were hanged by white vigilantes during that time. Benevolent societies provided health and economic services for blacks who were denied these services by white organizations.

After the town was incorporated, a large sawmill was built and operated by the Cane Lake Lumber Company. After the sawmill closed in 1909, other settlers began moving in and establishing farms and plantations. Most of the plantations were organized as small self-sustained, semi-closed communities with their own schools, churches, and homes. The plantations grew in number and economic wealth, using cheap agricultural labor provided by descendants of freed enslaved people, many of whom worked as sharecroppers, tenants, and wage laborers. After World War II, farm mechanization advanced rapidly, which led to the decline of plantation agriculture, including sharecropping, and there was a steady outmigration of blacks, who served as the chief source of cheap labor. However, during the 1950s and 1960s, black labor continued to serve as a dominant social, economic, and political force in Glendora and the surrounding areas. This period was marked by a slow decline in the plantation system, including sharecropping, as new labor-saving technology eliminated the vast majority of the agricultural workforce. Gradually, the "cotton kingdom" began to crumble as it lost the cheap labor of black people that had created wealth for white families.

Following the Brown v. Topeka Board of Education decision in 1954, the Civil Rights Movement triggered widespread social unrest in the area over the racial desegregation of public schools. There were also many protests and outrages over blatant violations of the civil rights of blacks by white vigilante groups such as the Ku Klux Klan. As the Civil Rights Movement grew and white resistance increased, white retaliation led to a series of lynches and murders. In 1955, the entire nation and world was traumatized by the brutal murder of a 14-year-old boy named Emmett Till, whose body was mutilated and thrown in the Black Bayou. Due to a series of events, including repercussions of school desegregation, increased voting rights of blacks, increased black political power, a massive fire that severely damaged the town, and black outrage created from the acquittal trial of two white men for the murder of Emmett Till, many whites abandoned their property in Glendora and moved away from the town.

The abandoned and dilapidated structures left by whites were sold to local African Americans. Robert Hilson, an African American, acquired and developed a significant number of the properties in Glendora, including the town district, and King's Place, a multi-purpose facility that included a café, juke joint, apartments, and auto mechanic shop. The out-migration of whites resulted in an overwhelming majority black population in Glendora. With a majority black population and growing interest in political participation, blacks were elected to a number of public offices. The town of Glendora was the first town in Tallahatchie County to elect black public officials. Thomas A. Williams was the first African American to serve on the Board of Alderman, and Henry L. Reese was elected the first African American mayor in 1976.

With roots in the plantation culture, writing and singing the Blues have been a tradition in Glendora and the Delta region. After Emancipation, many blues singers emerged in the area. Men and women sang the blues in juke joints that expressed and reflected their frustrations, relief, fears, and anxiety in their day-to-day life on the plantations or in the communities. Many of the blues singers performed at King's Place, which was known as the "Las Vegas" of Tallahatchie County. Aleck "Rice" Miller, also known as Sonny Boy William II, "King of the Blues harmonica," was a native of Glendora and often performed at the famous King's Place. As they say, "back in the day, King's Place was hopping."

As the Civil Rights Movement waned, several factors contributed to stifling of the local economy for black farmers and businesses in the town of Glendora, including the decline in farming due to out-migration of the working-age and middle class population, the high costs of mechanization of farming, closing of the Amtrak Railway Station, control of the allocation of revenue by the white power structure of Tallahatchie County, and the relocation of the main highway that isolated the town from potential vendors and visitors. The current 285 residents of the town were referred to as "the people left behind" because they decided not to leave the area. They remained behind because, as several of the elders say, "there is no place like home," and at home there is still hope for a brighter future.

Currently, Glendora sits on a 200-acre tract of land in the heart of the Mississippi Delta, along Highway 49 near the southern borderline of Tallahatchie County. Tallahatchie County is one of the 18 counties that comprise the Mississippi Delta region that stretches almost 200 miles along the eastern border of the Mississippi River from Memphis to Vicksburg. Although Glendora is located in one of the most impoverished regions of the country, it is a place where about 50 families call home. The population of Glendora declined from 561 in 1990 to 285 in 2000, a decrease by almost half (49%). Most of the residents were property owners and were still actively engaged in the production of commercial crops such as corn, rice, soybeans, and cotton. Nearly 60% of the residents of Glendora were youth under the age of 18.

Poverty runs deep and wide in Glendora. Some families have lived under impoverished conditions for many generations. According to the U.S. Census (2009), 80% of the residents of Glendora lived in poverty, with incomes below the poverty level, compared to 28% for the whole state. Almost two-thirds of the residents in poverty (74.1%) lived in rental properties. The poverty rate was highest among the 6-11, 16-17, and 25-34 age groups. The poverty rate for children was 86.1%, and 34.6% for people who did not graduate from high school (U.S. Census, 2009). Glendora has experienced little change in these conditions since 2009.

The high rate of inter-generational poverty, deteriorated infrastructure, lack of job opportunities, and the struggling educational system that exist today in Glendora and Tallahatchie County are remnants of the once dominated plantation system that created economic depression for many black families. Despite the high rate of poverty, 40% unemployment, deteriorating buildings, lack of sidewalks or curbs, abandoned buildings, and the nuisance of the Canadian National Railway trains that daily rumble through the center of the town, Glendora is making a valiant struggle to become a "stone of hope" for its citizens. The current Mayor of Glendora is Johnny B. Thomas, a native of the town, who was elected in 1982, following Henry Reese, who was elected the first African American

Mayor of Glendora in 1976. The following list of mayors of Glendora served from 1900 to the present.

Mayors of Glendora, 1900–Present

William Gay
1900–1939: He was the first mayor of Glendora, during the era of the establishment of a sawmill and expansion of large plantations by the Graham, Flautts, Bramlett, and Frederick families. This was also the period of black suppression by the black codes and neo–slavery sharecropping.

Marion E. Lowe
1939–1959: He was mayor during the Jim Crow era and during the abduction and murder of Emmett Till. He was instrumental in condemning one of his white employees that was accused of murdering a black man, Clinton Melton, and led the charge to run him out of town.

Nutty Moyers
Early 1960s: He was a Jewish merchant; all of the merchants of Glendora were of Jewish descent. Other Jewish families were the Levine, Cohen, Greensburg, and Cummings families. The Hodges kid was murdered by a white man.

Harold Moyer
Late 1960s: He became mayor during the civil rights era that resulted in the out-migration of Jewish merchants from the town, who sold their property to African Americans. There was cooperation between the Jewish and white residents of the community. He was mayor when an Asian child shot and killed an African American child that increased racial tension and conflict in the town.

Clifton Bishop
Late 1960s–Early 1970s: He was the last Caucasian mayor of Glendora, who was succeeded by an African American mayor.

Henry Reese   1976-1982: He was the first African American
                     to be elected mayor of Glendora during the
                     post-civil rights period. His tenure involved
                     much political and racial strife, including the
                     murder of the town clerk, Myrtle Hitch. He
                     resigned in the middle of his second term.

Johnny B. Thomas   1982-Present: He was the second African
                     American mayor of Glendora, elected after the
                     Civil Rights Movement when the town had
                     a majority black population. The only white
                     Alderman resigned. Thomas was threatened
                     by whites, who told him that he needed to be
                     floating down the Tallahatchie River.

CHAPTER 3

THE BURDEN OF SLAVERY

THE PEOPLE OF Glendora are descendants of enslaved people who were imported from African countries to work in the industries and plantations of America to generate wealth for their European-American owners. While slavery generated wealth and enriched the coffers of white families and institutions, it was a Maafa (a Swahili word that means great disaster) and burden for the enslaved Africans. Enslaved people who toiled on the plantations for over 200 years looked to the day when they could "lay my burden down," as expressed in the old Negro hymn "Lay My Burden Down, Lord." They looked to the day when they could "put on their long white robes, and shout all over heaven." Many of them would never live to see freedom from slavery on this side of heaven, and could only hope for a better life after death from the misery suffered here on earth as slaves in bondage.

During the 1700s and 1800s, cotton plantations in the Mississippi Delta were established by white settlers seeking to make their fortune in cotton production. They found an abundance of cheap land and brought enslaved African people with them to provide the main source of labor. With the enslaved Africans, land, money, and some knowledge of farming, the Mississippi Delta and the lower Mississippi River Valley were eventually transformed into the richest cotton-farming land in the country. From 1817 to 1860, Mississippi became the largest cotton-producing state in America, boosted by the use of enslaved laborers, who were captured in African countries, bought from slave traders by Europeans, and transported to America. Large plantations in the South were supported by a plantocracy of elite planters in alliance with the government and private banks and other institutions, which created a "cotton kingdom" that generated wealth from millions of enslaved Africans. Natchez, Mississippi played a significant role in the southward movement of the slave population to the waiting cotton plantations of the Deep South. The second largest slave market in the South, behind New Orleans (Congo Square), was located at Natchez. Enslaved Africans were bought and sold in these markets that provided slaves for Mississippi and the rest of the South. An outdoor exhibit of the slave market, called The Forks of The Road, is located in Natchez, Mississippi. By 1850, slavery had become the most dominant institution in the South that created some of the wealthiest people in the United States.

As a result of the international (African to America) and domestic slave trades, the enslaved population in Mississippi increased from about 3,489 in 1800 to 436,631 in 1860. With the use of enslaved laborers, the invention of the cotton gin in 1793, and the discovery of new higher producing varieties, cotton production increased from zero pounds in 1800 to 565 million pounds in 1859, which made Mississippi the leading producer of cotton in the United States, and Alabama ranking second with 441 million *pounds (*Source: *Cotton and the Growth of the American Economy: 1790-1860).* With enslaved laborers, cotton, land, and management, Mississippi became one of the wealthiest states in the nation. For almost three-fourths of a century, enslaved laborers on cotton plantations, endowed by nature with alluvial enriched land, created many wealthy white families, and at the same time created many impoverished black families. As such, cotton production on slave plantations was a "blessing" to some and a "curse" to others. Mississippi seceded from the Union in 1861 and suffered greatly from the loss of its plantations and slave property during and after the American Civil War.

Plantation owners of Tallahatchie County, where Glendora is located, purchased a portion of the enslaved people, who were brought into Mississippi to provide labor for the sprawling plantations. Based on Census records, in 1860, there was a total of 5,054 enslaved people in Tallahatchie County that represented 1.2 percent of the total

436,631 enslaved people in Mississippi. By 1860, there were more enslaved people in the State of Mississippi (436,631) than free white people (353,901). In addition, a total of 773 free people of color was listed in the U.S. Census (U.S. Census, 1860). Free people of color were mostly former enslaved people, who managed to purchase their freedom or who were manumitted (freed) by their owners. Many of the enslaved people and free people of color were the offspring or blood relatives of whites, created by forced sexual relations by white owners and workers with their slaves (called miscegenation). The 1860 Census listed 34 slaveholders, who owned the largest number of slaves in Tallahatchie County, compiled in a transcription conducted by Tom Blake (See table below). These 34 slaveholders accounted for 2,121 slaves, or 42% of the total slaves in Tallahatchie County. The rest of the slaves in the County were held by a total of 326 slaveholders.

Largest Slaveholders in Tallahatchie County, Mississippi, 1860

Name	Number of Slaves	Name	Number of Slaves
Allen, Abraham J.	46	Hunter, John B.	64
Bellamy, George W.	61	Johnson, Thomas G.	52
Bennett, Edward	37	Leigh, James	49
Bennett, Henry S.	49	Martin, Jackson	55
Bridges, Thomas J. N.	50	Means, D. J. & H. J.	93
Coleman, Richard	46	Murphy, Smith	42
Craig, James	71	Noel, John E.	34
Dickens, Samuel	38	Patterson, Alexander	75
Duncan, James M.	71	Pope, Spias	41
Fisher, Ephriam S.	51	Sharkley, Greenwood L.	78
Fleming, Reuben	83	Smith, Julia L.	81
Gilbert, William S.	40	Stovall, C. C.	80
Harper, James N.	80	Taylor, William J.	150
Harvey, George G.	51	Hawkins, John A.	65
Houston, James A.	50	Thornton, Philip H.	83
Thompson, Joseph W.	70	Wright, James C.	75

Sources: *The 1860 U.S. Census Slave Schedules for Tallahatchie County, Mississippi* (NARA microfilm series M653, Roll 603). Transcribed by Tom Blake, February 2002.

Mississippi Population, 1800–1860

Year	White	Free Colored	Slave	Total
1800★	5,179	182	3,489	8,850
1810★	23,024	240	17,088	40,352
1830	70,443	519	65,659	136,621
1840	179,074	1,366	195,211	375,651
1850	295,718	930	309,878	606,526
1860	353,901	773	436,631	791,305

★Mississippi Territory (present-day Mississippi and Alabama)
Source: *Cotton and the Growth of the American Economy: 1790-1860*

Mississippi Cotton Production, 1800–1859
(millions of pounds)

1800	0
1833	70
1839	193.2
1849	194
1859	535.1

Source: *Cotton and the Growth of the American Economy: 1790-1860*

In Tallahatchie County, an abundance of land and enslaved workers were the main ingredients used by plantation owners to create a great amount of wealth that went in the pockets and bank accounts of white owners, families, bankers, retail enterprises, and investors to fuel the economy of the South and the nation. In 1820, the *American Farmer* magazine estimated that a single slave could tend six acres of cotton and eight acres of corn. The prime cotton picker was a healthy 16 to 30 year old male, who could pick 500 or more pounds of cotton per day. During the heyday of cotton production in 1801 when cotton sold for 44 cents per pound, 500 pounds of cotton would yield $220 per day or $1,320 for a 6-day week or $5,280 per month. At this rate, 20 healthy slaves could generate a gross total of $422,400 for a four-month season, and 50 healthy slaves could generate a gross total of 1.06 million dollars for the owner

(Thomas Durant, *The Relevance and Applicability of the Marxian Theory of Capitalism to American Plantation Slavery*, Paper presented at the Sweat Equity Conference, Mississippi Valley State University, Itta Bena, MS, October 16–18, 2013).

Although a great amount of wealth was generated by enslaved laborers, the enslaved people received little or no benefit from this wealth. This vicious, violent, oppressive, and inhumane system lasted for more than 200 years and created abject poverty in the form of low income, poor education, poor health, social and economic deprivation, inequality, social injustice, and an underclass among African Americans. To a great extent, the negative effects of these conditions persist today in the Mississippi Delta in the form of high rates of poverty and substandard living. Many black people in Tallahatchie County still live with many of the social, economic and psychological ills that were created by the plantation system and culture that were maintained and perpetuated by laws and Jim Crow customs.

CHAPTER 4

LET MY PEOPLE GO

THESE WERE THE latter days of slavery in the land of America, in the year of our Lord and Savior, eighteen hundred and sixty, where, heretofore, slaves had been held in bondage for more than two hundred years. And during this period, great multitudes were captured from the lands of Africa, from the tribes of Wolof, Serer, Mandinke, Bambara, Fulani, Hausa, Ewe, Mende, Ibo, Yoruba, Twi, Ga, and many more, and sold as chattel, and herded like cattle into the belly of ships in chains. And millions did suffer and cry out in great pain, and died from the wretched journey. And the dead were strewn into the great depths of the ocean, their bodies coming to rest in a graveyard of water at the bottom of the Atlantic that formed a line of tombs, spanning thousands of miles, from the coast of Africa to the coast of the Americas.

And enslaved Africans were held captives and forced into bondage and did labor and toil under heavy burdens, in the farms and factories of the North and in the cotton, sugar cane, tobacco, and rice plantations of the South. And the Revolutionary War was fought, and colonial America won its independence from the British. And more and more land was conquered from the Native Americans, as America expanded its boundaries southward and westward.

17

And a Declaration of Independence was penned, which inscribed these words, as a proclamation to the free:

> We hold these truths to be self-evident, that all men are created equal, that they are endowed by their Creator with certain unalienable rights, that among these are life, liberty and the pursuit of happiness.

But the law of the land, emanated from the hearts of men, professed by their tongues, inscribed by their hands, declared by their power, and enforced by their rule, that slaves were chattel, and therefore, not human beings, and thus, had no right to the freedoms of the land.

And the rulers of the nation drafted a great constitution by which to govern the people of the United States of America, which proclaimed these words:

> We the people of the United States, in order to form a more perfect union, establish justice, insure domestic tranquility, provide for the common defense, promote the general welfare, and secure the blessings of liberty to ourselves and our posterity, do ordain and establish this Constitution for the United States of America.

And this was done on the seventeenth day of September, seventeen hundred and eighty-seven, in the year of our Lord and Savior, by the hands of 39 men, from among whom a leader named George Washington would be chosen. But again the law of the land, driven by the will of men, who were descendants of Europeans, from a foreign land, who came to America to seek freedom from religious and political persecution, yet declared by their power, and the force of their might that slaves were chattel, and not humans, and therefore, were not entitled to the rights, freedom, and dignity which they claimed for themselves.

And John Adams succeeded George Washington as president; and Thomas Jefferson succeeded Adams; and James Madison succeeded Jefferson; and James Monroe succeeded Madison; and John Quincy Adams succeeded Monroe; and Andrew Jackson succeeded John

Quincy Adams; and Martin Van Buren succeeded Jackson; and William Harrison succeeded Van Buren; and John Tyler succeeded Harrison; and James Polk succeeded Tyler; and Zachary Taylor succeeded Polk; and Millard Fillmore succeeded Taylor; and Franklin Pierce succeeded Fillmore; and James Buchanan succeeded Pierce; and Abraham Lincoln succeeded Buchanan. And all the years of these presidents, who reigned over the independent United States of America, during the period of slavery in the new republic, were nine and eighty years.

And during this period, abolitionists pleaded, argued, and fought for the freedom of the slaves; and a few slaves did escape to the North and to Canada through the Underground Railroad. And heroes of great valor, men and women, fought against slavery and led a few from bondage to freedom: Harriet Tubman, Nat Turner, John Brown, Frederick Douglass, and Sojourner Truth. But the hearts of the slavers were hardened, and they refused to let my people go.

And in the eighty-ninth year of the reign of the independent republic of the United States, a man named Abraham Lincoln rose to power. After much toil, trials, and tribulations, Lincoln made a proclamation for the emancipation of the slaves. But the rulers of the southern states would not yield because satan had embellished their desire for greed and profit, and hardened their hearts. And they refused to let my people go.

And the northern and southern states became divided over the issue of slavery. And the South chose as its leader, a man named Jefferson Davis, to lead the Confederacy of Southern States, and repulse the intervention, and defy the proclamation of Lincoln, who reigned in the North, to free the slaves. And Lincoln pleaded and made propositions to compensate slave owners for their slaves, if they would free the slaves from bondage. But in the vast plantation system of the Southern Confederacy, the roots of slavery had become firmly implanted like the mighty live oak tree that resist the wind and the storm, and shout back with great disdain, I shall not be moved! And the hearts of the slavers were defiant and hardened; and they refused to let my people go.

And the slaves did work, sing, and pray, with great hope, in secrecy to their God, that they one day would be free:

"Nobody knows the trouble I see, nobody knows but Jesus."

"Steal away, steal away, steal away to Jesus, for I ain't got long to stay here."

"Above my head, I hear music in the air; there must be a God somewhere."

"Go down Moses, way down in Egypt land; and tell ole Pharos (massah), to let my people go.

And God heard their cry, and was angered at the misdeeds of the slavers and removed his favor from them. And a mighty war was fought in the land, and 529,332 were killed, the like of which has never before or since been witnessed; not in the Revolutionary War, where 25,342 were killed; or the War of 1812, where 2,260 were killed; or the Mexican War, where 13,283 were killed; or the Spanish American War, where 2,446 were killed; or World War I, where 116,516 were killed; or World War II, where 405,399 were killed; or the Korean War, where 54,246 were killed; or the Vietnam War, where 56,480 were killed; And all of them that were killed in these wars totaled one million, two hundred five thousand, three hundred and four, not counting the enemies who were killed.

And slaves fought and died alongside free men on both sides, against each other in many battles, great and small; at Fort Sumter; at Vicksburg; at Bull Run; at Antietam; at Frederickburg; at Chancellorville; at Gettysburg; at Port Hudson; at Chickamauga; at Petersburg; at Cedar Creek; at Cedar Mountain; at Five Forks; at Fort Henry; at Malvern Hill; at Mechanicsville; at Mobile Bay; at Monitor and Merrimac; at Murfreesboro; at Nashville; at New Orleans; at Petersburg; at Spottsylvania; and at the Battle of the Wilderness. And the war did rage on for four years. And when the suffering became very great, and the will to fight was weakened, the soldiers laid down their arms and the Southern Confederacy reluctantly surrendered to the Union of the North.

And in the year eighteen hundred sixty-three, in the year of our Lord, before the end of the Civil War between the North and the South, Lincoln sent out to all the states under his authority, a proclamation for the emancipation of all slaves from their captors, which proclaimed these words:

That on the 1ˢᵗ day of January, 1863, all persons held as slaves within any State or designated part of a State the people whereof shall then be in rebellion against the United States shall be then, thenceforward, and forever free.

And almost two years later when the proclamation was heard by the mass of the slaves, there was great jubilation among them. An old African preacher named Rue led the throng in, "Sound the loud timber o'ver Egypt's dark sea, Jehovah has triumphed, his people are free." And they gave thanks to the Lord, and wept, and shouted, and sang with joy, "Blow ye the Trumpet Blow," for God has moved a mighty hand upon their captors, and forced them to lay down their weapons, and surrender in body, if not in spirit. And God answered their prayers for freedom from bondage. And my people were let go!

And a massive exodus of ex-slaves from the plantations did occur. And wave after wave of slaves, some four million in number, marched out of the plantations to freedom from their captors. And with their freedom, they began to build new lives, with all of the hope, energy, strength, and meager resources they could salvage. And they made their way into the wilderness of a strange and still hostile land.

And this is the truth as I know it, which has been handed down from generation to generation. And let all of God's people, believe and know all that which is true, for it is written in the Word of God, to know the truth, and it shall make you free.

Despite the abolishment of slavery, racial oppression endured in Mississippi. Although blacks outnumbered whites in the Delta, whites controlled a disproportionately higher amount of the wealth and power in the area, which continues to this day. After Emancipation, ex-slaves and their descendants struggled with oppressive white planters over land and human rights.

CHAPTER 5

THE BLACK CODES AND JIM CROW

FTER THE CIVIL War, the passage of the 13th Amendment to the U.S. Constitution brought legalized freedom to approximately three million black southerners, who were landless, and possessed little money and economic resources to support themselves. After Emancipation, white business owners and employers realized that they could not support their businesses or maximize their wealth without cheap, submissive, and non-threatening black labor. Thus, in response to Emancipation, Southern states legislated a system of Black Codes to "keep the Negro in his place," socially, economically, and politically.

The State of Mississippi was the first state to create Black Codes shortly after the Civil War in 1865. Although these codes were stated in legal jargon, they attempted to control, limit, or reduce the freedom and rights of blacks in several areas: vagrant laws to control social movements; civil rights laws to control access to public facilities; apprentice laws to control black laborers; and penal laws that spelled out punishment for violations of certain social customs. These laws were part of a larger system created by Southern whites to suppress the freedom of newly emancipated African American slaves that restricted them to low-wage jobs and indebtedness. Actually, the Black Codes were a new form of slavery. In part, the Mississippi Black Codes stipulated that,

All freedmen, free negroes and mulattoes over the age of
eighteen years, found on the second Monday in January,
1866, or thereafter, without lawful employee or business,
or found unlawfully assembling themselves together, either
in the day or night time, all white persons so assembling
themselves with freedmen, free negroes, or mulattoes,
or usually associating with freedmen, free negroes or
mulattoes, on terms of equality, or living in adultery or
fornication with a freed woman, free negro or mulatto,
shall be deemed vagrants, and on conviction thereof shall
be fined a sum not exceeding, in the case of a freedmen,
free negro, or mulatto, fifty dollars, and a white man
two hundred dollars, and imprisoned, at the discretion
of the court, the free negro not exceeding ten days, and
the white man not exceeding six months (http://chnm.
gmu /courses/122/ recon/code.html, 1/18/16, p. 3).

According to the vagrancy code, blacks were required to present,
every January, proof of employment, with violations punishable by
arrest (for which the arresting officer would be paid $5, to be taken
from the wages of the arrestee). All blacks who could not pay a
special tax levied against blacks 18 to 60 years old, could be arrested
for vagrancy. Similar to the fugitive slave laws, the vagrancy law
mandated the return of runaway workers and loss of their job for the
year. The law was amended to include punishment for sympathetic
whites. Another law authorized the state to take custody of children
whose parents could or would not support them, and the children
"apprenticed" to their former owners. The law stated that,

Black children under the age of 18, within their respective
counties, beats, or districts who are orphans, or whose
parent or parents have not the means, or who refuse to
provide for and support said minors; and thereupon it
shall be the duty of said Probate Court to order the clerk
of said court to apprentice said minors to some competent
and suitable person, on such terms as the court may direct,
having a particular care to the interest of said minors (http://
chnm.gmu/courses/122/recon/code.html, 1/18/16, p. 1).

These children could be disciplined with corporal punishment, and if they escaped could be re-captured and imprisoned if they resisted. Under the codes, blacks were prevented from buying liquor and carrying weapons, with the penalty involving "hiring out" for labor with no pay. Other laws made it unlawful for blacks and whites to intermarry, with a sentence of life in prison for conviction; deemed co-habitation of a black man and woman as constituting a legal marriage; blacks could be a witness against another black person in civil and criminal cases, but could not be a witness against whites; forfeiture of wages for quitting their job; and inflict punishment upon a black employee by a white employer. It is noteworthy that for every black code that addressed a law for blacks, there was a corresponding benefit for whites, in one form or another, socially, economically, or legally (http://chnm. gmu/courses/122/recon/code.html, 1/18/16, p.1-8).

The Black Codes were the predecessors of the Jim Crow laws and customs that defined the doctrine of racism, racial prejudice, racial segregation, and race relations. The effects of the Black Codes lingered in the American society long after the emancipation of enslaved Africans, often in the form of Jim Crow customs designed for the social and economic suppression of the rights of black people. One such incidence occurred during the 1960s. Mrs. Lillian Mitchell was the first African American to operate a racially integrated restaurant in Glendora. Prior to opening her restaurant, she was a cook and domestic household worker for white families. Both black and white patrons were frequent customers at her restaurant, including Jewish merchants of the town and the surrounding area. Her hamburgers and stew were second to none.

One day a young Caucasian woman came to the restaurant and began co-mingling with the black patrons. A young Caucasian woman who worked next door to the restaurant did not like the racial mixing and called a deputy sheriff, who was her brother-in-law, to come to the restaurant and remove the young Caucasian woman. When the deputy arrived at the restaurant, an African American man named Bailey attempted to verbally defend the young white woman to prevent her from being jailed for no reason than mixing with the black patrons. In the South, especially in Mississippi, it was against Jim Crow customs for blacks and whites to co-mingle in a public or private place. Because Bailey intervened in the matter, the deputy struck him on the head with his weapon that caused a gaping wound and severe bleeding. Bailey was an African American land owner, farmer, and carpenter, with a wife and seven children.

Another incidence occurred after the Voters Rights Act was passed in 1965. Even after blacks gained the right to vote, some plantation owners threatened to fire them if they registered to vote. During that time, black people still were forced to give deference and respect to white people without getting any in return. The Jim Crow customs were designed to keep black people subservient to white people and to exploit black labor for the social and economic benefit of white families. The black codes were also designed to maintain racial segregation of public and private facilities and separate and unequal facilities that relegated blacks to second class citizenship. The Ku Klux Klan was one of the white supremacy groups whose main goal was to maintain white dominance and racial segregation through acts of violence and intimidation, including murders, lynchings, hangings, whippings, and arson.

During the Civil Rights Movement, Blacks fought for voting rights, school desegregation, equal rights, social justice, and anti-discrimination laws, which threatened white power and privileges. Some whites responded by forming vigilante, hate, and violent groups such as the Ku Klux Klan and the White Citizens Council. Mississippi was the last state in the South to integrate public schools and permit blacks to vote. In absolute measures, it cannot be denied that the town of Glendora and the Mississippi Delta have come a long ways from where it used to be, but in relative measures, it still is a long way from the rest of the State and nation. In the 21st century, new movements have emerged to continue the transformation process toward the creation of a New Mississippi Delta, including the town of Glendora and the county of Tallahatchie. Only time will tell if these movements will be successful and if the people of Tallahatchie County and other parts of the Delta can rise further above the circumstances of their past.

CHAPTER 6

SHARECROPPING:
A NEW FORM OF SLAVERY

AFTER SLAVERY WAS abolished by the 13th Amendment in December 1865, almost three million people of African descent were left impoverished, many for life, and almost half a million "free" people of color were not much better off. Unfortunately, many of the freed blacks who were too old, poor, or indoctrinated to leave, remained on the plantations as sharecroppers, tenants, or laborers. Ideally, sharecropping was a system of agriculture in which a landowner permitted a tenant to use the land for crop production in exchange for a share of the crop produced on that land. However, the form of sharecropping that was put in place immediately after slavery legally ended was actually a new form of slavery. Many of the freed slaves had no education or economic resources for survival and were forced to continue working on the plantation of their former owners as sharecroppers. Due to fraud, high interest rates, inclement weather, and abusive tactics, almost invariably black sharecroppers ended up in debt to the land owner, and the Black Codes/laws made it illegal for them to leave the plantation without paying off their debt. If they left without paying off their debt, they could be arrested and sent back to the land owner and forced to work without pay or they could become a part of the penal system and be forced to work without pay as a part of the convict labor system.

Actually, sharecroppers were just a little more than enslaved workers, who worked hard and made subsistence wages or incomes from their crops. If they had a good crop year they could break even or earn barely enough to cover their cost of living. If the crop failed or the plantation owner cheated them out of their "fair" share, then they received nothing for their labor. Most of the large plantations had a plantation store that gave "credit" to the farm hands to buy food and supplies from the store that he owned. If the workers could not pay their debt to the plantation store owner, they had to stay and try to work their way out of debt the next year. In many instances, it was a losing cause because the plantation owner kept the records on the debt of the workers. It was like double jeopardy because if the weather or crop disease didn't get you, the plantation owner did. Many sharecroppers ended up in debt for life. Although most black workers had the wisdom to know when they were being cheated, the Jim Crow customs forbade them from challenging the plantation owner because they could lose their job and be evicted from their plantation shack. It was against Jim Crow customs to "get out of their place" and dispute the word of their white boss or plantation owner.

My mother and father were sharecroppers just as many of the black families were in Tallahatchie County. My mother once worked as a sharecropper in the fields, hoeing and picking cotton on the Flautts plantation where John Milam was the overseer. Milam once came into our house and beat my mother in front of her children to force her to go to work in the fields, in spite of the fact that she told him that she was sick and unable to work. As one of her children at the time, I witnessed this act of abuse and cruelty to my mother. This is how black people were treated on many of the plantations, and as late as the 1960s, black sharecroppers were still under a form of bondage. Due to the harsh treatment of my mother and other workers that I witnessed with my own eyes, I developed a hatred for working for the white man on the plantations, and looked for every opportunity to escape this cruel form of existence and become an entrepreneur to operate my own business. Eventually, through many trials and tribulations, I would succeed. However, it would be a struggle because as Frederick Douglass once stated, without struggle, there is no progress.

Sharecropping continued to exploit the labor of black workers for the benefit of the plantation owners and their families long after Emancipation and long after the 13th Amendment was passed, that granted freedom to enslaved people. Thus, generations of black families were further impoverished by this new form of slavery. The oppressive conditions of slavery and sharecropping were a major reason for the massive exodus or out-migration of blacks from the rural South to large cities in the North, Midwest, and West. Many of the older family members in Glendora were sharecroppers or descendants of families that were sharecroppers on plantations in the area. Some of the plantations in Tallahatchie County and the surrounding area that depended on sharecroppers and black laborers to cultivate and harvest their crops and tend their livestock were Frederick, Graham, Bramlett, Flautts, Sturdivant, Buford, and Equen. On some of the larger plantations, black men were hired to keep the black workers under control. Usually, black men did the heavy work on the plantations and black women did the domestic work in the house of the white owners. Black women who worked in the "big house" on the plantation were sometimes sexually abused. I recall that in my community, white plantation owners had children by some of the black domestic women that produced mixed-race or mulatto babies.

In rural Tallahatchie County and other parts of the South, especially prior to 1960, blacks had no rights that the white man was required to respect. The strongest black men who stood up for their rights were eradicated. These were black men who willfully or unwillfully violated, defied, or questioned the Jim Crow laws and customs of the land. These Jim Crow customs evolved from the slave codes that were established by plantation owners during slavery that defined the "dos" and "don'ts" for enslaved people. These codes were designed to control the conduct of the "Negroes." Although the strongest and most resistant black men and women were eliminated or controlled by lynching, whipping, fear, and deprivation, the white man did not believe that it was rational, economical, or even possible to eliminate or kill all of the Negroes because by doing so would eliminate their main source of labor, their wealth, and their livelihood. Thus, the white man and the black man were locked into a vicious cycle of mutual dependence, with unequal rights and a skewed distribution of wealth, power, privileges, freedom, justice, and equality. One could say that the South, in general, and the plantations, in particular, were doomed by their institution of the Black Codes that kept the whole society from advancing by enculturing fear, emotional insecurity, and impoverishment for blacks.

Unfortunately, sharecropping lasted about 100 years in Mississippi and the South from 1865 to the 1960s. Spurred by the Civil Rights Movement and the Civil Rights Act of 1964, combined with agricultural mechanization and industrialization, blacks began to leave the plantations in the South, especially after World War II. There was a massive out-migration of blacks from plantations in the Tallahatchie County area, including Sturdivant, Buford, Equen, Frederick, Flautts, Lowe, Alexander, Dale, and Reynolds plantations. Some blacks were able to acquire farms of their own, some moved to Glendora and other small towns in the surrounding area, and others moved to Jackson, Mississippi or other cities outside the State. They were not only fleeing the hard life on the plantations, but also trying to find a better quality of life for their families. As a result of these changes, many of the large plantations turned to corporate farming and some closed for good.

In his book, *Up from Slavery*, Booker T. Washington provides a detailed account of what it was like to be free from slavery without an education, a home, or a means of livelihood. Washington believed that education and economic self-sufficiency were the key to finding a pathway out of poverty, but how to get it was the challenge. Many of the freed blacks formed communities near the plantations where they or their ancestors were enslaved or had labored. In time, they built houses, churches, schools, and businesses. Glendora, like other rural communities in the Delta, emerged from these inauspicious conditions. The Mississippi Delta was one of the areas that suffered from the brunt of the oppressive conditions of enslavement and sharecropping, which created one of the most impoverished classes and regions in the South and in the country. Without free or cheap labor to generate wealth, Mississippi became one of the poorest states in the nation. It is quite tragic that the counties where the richest cotton plantations were located became some of the poorest counties in the nation.

Sharecroppers and low-wage laborers replaced enslaved field laborers and domestic household workers replaced house slaves. Many sharecroppers never saw a profit from their work because they were subjected to a new form of "slavery"—denial of basic rights, privileges, and social justice. With no future in sharecropping, oppressive socioeconomic conditions, and the decline in cotton production due to mechanized farming, vast numbers of blacks moved from the Delta to Memphis, Chicago, and other cities in the North, West, and Mid-West in search for a better way of life. Between 1910 and 1970, 6.5 million blacks left the South and moved north. Many blacks from the Mississippi Delta were included in that number. Mississippi and other southern states became the major battleground of the Civil Rights Movement that was energized in 1955 by the murder of Emmett Till in Tallahatchie, Leflore County, and Glendora.

CHAPTER 7

THE JOHNNY B. THOMAS STORY
From Sharecropping to Mayor of Glendora

THIS IS THE story of Johnny B. Thomas and how he rose from a sharecropper's family to Mayor of the town of Glendora.

I am Johnny B. Thomas, Mayor of Glendora since 1982. I am one of the "people left behind" referred to by the U.S. National Commission on Rural Poverty in the late 1960s. I did not leave Glendora and move to Memphis, Chicago, Detroit, L.A. or one of the other large cities in the North, Midwest or West like so many of the former residents of this area. I can't say that I blame them for leaving Glendora to improve their quality of life and increase the opportunities for their advancement. But if Dr. King's prophecy is true, then there must be people who are willing to stay in this town to create hope and eliminate conditions that created the "mountain of despair" that has characterized our past. Actually, the people who moved away did not leave me behind in Glendora; I decided to stay and meet my fortune or fate right here where I was born; right here where my ancestors lived and died. We have land, we have homes, we have families, we have freedom, and we have the will to create a better community and place in which to live. We must find a way to create jobs and career opportunities to keep our youth from leaving the area. Too often, our youth leave the area after graduating from high school, and even before, if their families decide to move away.

This area has lost so many young people who could have been the leaders and future of this community. They left behind the less educated, the poor, and the elderly, in search of a brighter future than their parents and grandparents had.

I was born on November 30, 1953, in rural Tallahatchie County to Adeline Hill and Henry Lee Loggins. My family was poor. Both of my parents had little education and my father could not read or write. I have often asked myself why was I born in Tallahatchie County, in this economically depressed and impoverished area? Why did God leave me here while so many others before me were murdered at the hands of vicious and violent white people? And how did I escape death when black men, women, and children around me were brutally lynched or murdered? I was two years old when Emmett Till was murdered, right near the community of Glendora where I lived. I heard the elders talking about Emmett Till and many other blacks who were murdered by whites for simple acts of disobedience or violation of Jim Crow laws and customs. I know for a fact that I have often walked in the shadow of death, but somehow avoided death by evil white people and sometimes enraged black people. I lived in a place where the culture of violence was all too common. I believe that my survival is due to divine intervention from angels that God sent to watch over me as I slept, slumbered, and walked through danger, known and unknown, seen and unseen. I have been protected by God's divine intervention because He still has a purpose for my life. I believe that I was left here to tell my story to help educate, motivate, and inspire others, to help in the healing of the people from past atrocities, and to help create a stone of hope for a brighter future for the descendants of the people of Glendora.

I was raised by my mother, along with three siblings, on the Flautts plantation, after my father, thought to be a witness in the Emmett Till murder, secretly left town in 1955 to avoid testifying against the two white men charged with the murder of Till. Thus, from around age three to age 15, I was raised by my mother on the Flautts plantation, where we were sharecroppers. Sharecropping was a vicious system of exploitation that was enforced by a culture of oppression, poverty, ignorance, and Jim Crow customs. Sharecropping was hard work with little pay that sometimes left us in debt to the plantation owner, if we had a bad crop. I barely attended school at an early age because education was not a high priority to sharecroppers because primary attention was given to making a living. If we did not make a good crop, then the livelihood of me and my family was in jeopardy. Thus, I never attended school regularly. When I did attend school, I was always able to catch up quickly because I was a quick learner. I could read and spell well and was good in mathematics, even prior to attending school. In this regard, I was a gifted kid.

The Flautts plantation where we lived had its own commissary, which allowed us to buy clothes and food on credit until we harvested the crops. We always prayed for a good crop so that the family would not go hungry. Many of our meals consisted of some combination of eggs, onions, milk, corn bread, and molasses made from sugar and water. Once I almost burned the house down and severely burned my face trying to make homemade syrup. Sometimes we had special meals of canned meats, cheese, rice, and powdered eggs that were commodities or subsidies distributed to poor families by the U.S. Department of Agriculture.

As I grew older, I had to take on additional responsibilities to help provide for the family. I worked in the fields picking and chopping cotton. As a youth, I worked for wages of 50 cents to 75 cents per hour, and earned about six dollars a day or 30 dollars a week. It did not take long before I found out that I did not want to live my life as a cotton picker or field worker on one of the plantations as most blacks did. I certainly did not want to be a sharecropper. Sharecropping was not only grueling work, but it was just a little higher than an enslaved worker. I hated plantation work and looked for every opportunity to leave the plantation. I found that opportunity when we moved from the Flautts plantation to a house across the street from the King's Place Juke Joint. My mother got a job working at at King's Place and, unfortunately, for me this was my escape from the plantation. At seven years of age, I began working at the King's Place Cafe with my mother to earn money to help support the family. I did cleaning and maintenance chores. By this time, my mother had five children to care for.

My mother and her children moved from the Bob and Ruth Flautts plantation around 1968 when I was 15 years old. Amazingly, as a single parent, she mustered up enough money to purchase a lot from Rose Cohn, a member of the Jewish community, who was moving from the town and sold all of her property to blacks. My mother purchased an old house from the Sturdivant plantation, and renovated it for her family. My family was the first to own their own business and home in the downtown area of Glendora. I recall how happy and overjoyed I was for moving off the plantation and into our own house. We were looked upon as "big shots" and some of the other families were jealous of my mother's accomplishment. I don't know how she managed to make this great accomplishment in a time of widespread poverty in our family. She was a very determined "pit bull" woman who worked hard to support her children.

At the age of 11, I was managing the juke joint. I learned how to operate the cash register, make change, ring up an order, and make a sale. I learned how to meet the customers' needs and demands for food, drinks, and entertainment. I learned how to set up and manage card games, black jack tables, billiards, and dice games, and ensure that the house got a cut of the gains from the gamblers. I even learned how to gamble myself and became one of the best billiard players in the area. I worked among many unsavory people, among people who occasionally killed or maimed each other, womanizers, and family wreckers. I knew all of the men who had outside women and children, and I thought this was what I should do as a man. I observed people gambling all of their hard-earned money away, having babies outside their family, and neglecting their families. This environment and behavior created a culture of instant sexual gratification to compensate for the oppressive treatment that black men received from whites.

When I was age 14, my mother married Jim Hill and their marriage lasted until his death when he was in his late 70s. However, they were separated for most of that time because he was in prison for the murder of two men in Glendora. One of the murders was allegedly over a woman, who was my mother, Adeline Hill. Jim and Adeline had no children. My mother exposed me to six men during her many relationships with different men over the years. The most memorable one was my father, Henry Lee Loggins, who was rumored to be an accomplice in the murder of Emmett Till.

I was stabbed twice in brawls at the club, and in one incident, was nearly fatally stabbed to death in a gambling event around the age of 13. I was never taken to the doctor and it is a wonder that I survived. Prior to age 16, I had seen three deaths. I learned how to defend myself in a juke joint atmosphere among hard-core drinking, dancing, and entertainment by blues singers, amidst womanizers, and man hunters. By age 14, I had become a straight out hustler and refused to go to school.

I never wanted to work on the plantation as a farm hand, cotton picker, house boy, laborer, or sharecropper. I did not want to abide by the hard-core black codes that existed on the plantations, nor did I want my independence, dignity, and manhood to be subjugated or controlled by the white man. Thus, at a very early age, I had a strong desire to become self-employed and work for myself. Although becoming self-employed did not guarantee me a life free from oppression by whites, at least I could gain some sense of independence, dignity, and manhood by being my own boss. Under the widespread oppressive economic conditions in Tallahatchie County, I felt that the less oppressive position was to be self-employed. Being self-employed was not an easy feat to accomplish because it meant that I would need the necessary revenue to become an entrepreneur. I would need business knowledge and expertise, capital, management skills, and labor, the same things that the white folks needed to operate their plantations, but without the system of violence and oppression that were common in the plantation system.

I thought about what business venture I could be successful in. Farming or agriculture was out because I would not be able to control the means of production. My reasoning was that I had to create a business out of the culture of the people in the area. I needed knowledge of the demand and supply for certain goods and services among the people of the community. I learned from observations that in Glendora, there was a desire and demand for alcohol and a place to socialize after a hard day of work on the plantations in the surrounding areas. Men needed some place to let off some steam, demonstrate their manhood, share life stories, enjoy entertainment, and even release pent up emotions by womanizing, dancing, and gambling, that unfortunately led to fist fights, cuttings, and killings, occasionally. Surrounded by plantations, people took the little they had to come to Glendora to celebrate life. We laid all of our troubles down for a while. Despite these disadvantages, the surrounding culture of the area created the opportunity for entrepreneurship for us to operate a juke joints and sell corn whiskey. Actually, they both go together.

I gained business knowledge and experience from working with my mother in a juke joint, from age seven to teenage. At the age of 17, I opened my own business that included a snack bar/restaurant and pawn shop. As a young man, I ran a hamburger shack for a few years and managed a clothes pawn shop and a liquor store. Later, I observed that people needed food and insurance, so I ventured into a grocery store, a merchandise store, and a life insurance business. I did all of this to make a living for me and my family. I also gained some knowledge about how to operate a business when I attended Mississippi Valley State University. However, I learned the practical knowledge and skills of business management from my cousin, Willie James Stewart, who was a businessman in Glendora. I continued my interest in business by opening a restaurant. In 1972, at the age of 19, I married the former Ella Rean Johnson.

Once conditions improved and blacks gained the right to vote and hold public office, I had a desire to run for a public office. My interest in holding a public office was to gain a position where I could help the people of the community and also help build the community. The businesses that I developed provided a social and economic base to support a campaign for public office. At age 22, I threw my hat into the game of politics and ran for the position of Constable in 1975. However, I had to give up my job as an employee of the county in order to run for Constable. Fortunately, I won the election as Constable. As a law enforcement officer, it appeared that some people attempted to make me a scapegoat by trying to use me to stir up disorder in the African American community. I was accused of trying to incite anger and unrest against law enforcement officers in the African American community. I worked hard to provide fairness to the citizens that had not realized that the office of Constable had the potential of assisting people to get the help they needed for their families and community. After I was elected Constable, I changed the way the office was operated and eliminated the harassment of people with traffic tickets, which was the practice of the past officer.

The movement for voter registration and desegregation of public schools and facilities that occurred during the1950s and 1960s, created an unsettling fear among whites, who strongly opposed racial integration of public schools and other public facilities. Whites feared that racial integration of public schools would order their children to attend the same schools with blacks. Another fear by whites was that if blacks gained and exercised the right to vote, they would gain political and economic power, and ultimately take control of the economic resources of the area. Although it would take a long hard battle to bring about significant changes in the racial, economic, and political order of Glendora, whites could see the "hand writing on the wall" that social and political changes were coming! In 1954 in a land mark decision, the U.S. Supreme ruled that racial segregation of public schools was unconstitutional.

Believing that blacks would eventually gain access to public facilities and public offices, whites began a rapid flight from Glendora and southern Tallahatchie County. Many whites abandoned their property and businesses, cut their losses, and fled from the area. Some whites sold their land and homes to blacks or anyone with the interest and money to buy them. Whites took with them the lion's share of the capital and commercial resources and assets that attracted investors to the town. Almost overnight, Glendora became a ghost town with a majority black population and a high rate of poverty. Within a short period, Glendora changed from 54% to 99% black. The only white resident listed for the town was a white plantation owner, who actually lived outside of the town, but had a Glendora address.

After holding the position of Constable for four years, in 1980, I was elected to the position of Alderman of the town of Glendora. As Alderman, I was a part of the legislative body that conducted the official business for the town, which gave me a voice in the governance of the town. However, as Alderman, I had little influence over the allocation of funds to Glendora and other towns in Tallahatchie County. I knew that without adequate funds, the town of Glendora could not grow and develop. The power to make allocation of funds to towns in the county was in the hands of the County Supervisor. This was the main reason that I decided to run for the position of County Supervisor in District 4 in 1980.

I ran for County Supervisor three times but each time lost to a Caucasian, despite the fact that Tallahatchie County was about 87% black. The last time I ran for County Supervisor I lost the election by only four or five votes. With the assistance of Attorneys Victor McTeer, Solomon Osborne, and Willie Perkins, I filed a law suit challenging the results and denial of appointment. An investigation of the election was conducted which found that 93 people voted illegally, prior to the opening of the polls at 7:00 a.m. All of these votes were for my opponent. Most of these votes were cast by black people who were intimidated by their white employers who told them that they had to show up for work on voting day or they would lose their jobs. After the 93 illegal votes were eliminated, I was declared the winner of the election and became the first African American County Supervisor of Tallahatchie County.

However, my election to the position of County Supervisor was short lived. As a ploy against me, to prevent me from serving in the position I was accused and convicted of owning and operating gambling machines. They engaged in a conspiracy to commit me to prison utilizing two convicted persons to accuse me of taking money to allow them to place gaming machines in the town. Several youth were also coerced by an African American deputy to inform the Sheriff that I was selling alcohol to minors. As a result, I was incarcerated for a federal misdemeanor crime without a trial, based on this charge by black henchmen of the white Sheriff. Consequently, I was stripped of my position, and incarcerated in a federal prison for four months for a state misdemeanor, while others who committed the same offense were charged a 100 dollar fine and spent no time in prison. Now, I was a black man with a criminal offense, even though it was a misdemeanor. After spending four months in prison, I was released from prison without any explanation or redress of my grievances.

The Election Commission was operated like a plantation. A lot of things were run that way in Tallahatchie County. It mattered who your friends were, and who you knew, more than what the rules were. So, it's that way in rural Mississippi. But some of us fought for our rights, even during earlier times, despite the looming danger of being murdered or lynched. A case in point was the courageous black men who formed a group called "The Magnificent Seven," who pushed for black political participation by boycotting stores and schools, with assistance from the NAACP and other county residents during the 1960s, which contributed to the election of blacks in positions such as mayors, aldermen, constables, county supervisors, sheriffs, and judges in the area. The Magnificent Seven were black men from the Thomas, Meeks, Huddleston, Little, Gardner, Kenniel, and Willis families, who protested against racial discrimination by boycotting local businesses. Individuals from the Hawkins, Baskins, Thomas, Spates, Whitaker, Tyler, Lee, Melton, Hilson, and Walker families established the Benevolent Aide and Burial Society, which provided social and economic aid to black families.

In 1982, at the age of 30, I decided to run for the office of Mayor of Glendora that brought new challenges. I had to fight the forces of racial discrimination by white folks, who dominated and controlled the public offices of Glendora since its origin. I also had to fight some of the black folks who had been brainwashed by whites to think that everyone "white" was right or who were dependent on white politicians and their connection with white plantation owners, who they worked for and who controlled their livelihood. At that time, many blacks did not register to vote because they feared that they would be evicted from the plantation, catch hell from their white boss, or worse yet, get fired. I was challenged by the mind-set of some blacks to remain meek and humble and just let the white man run the government as he always had—a don't buck the system attitude, just learn to survive in it. Because I was outspoken for the rights of blacks to vote and run for public office, and was not afraid to speak truth to the white power structure, I was labeled a radical by whites and some blacks. Although I was continuously harassed by the police, I was elected Mayor of Glendora, making me the second African American to hold this position.

Shortly after being elected, the Sheriff Department began harassing me. The Sheriff seized all of my stock (food, liquor and merchandise) from my business and took it to the judge's office. These items were never returned and were consumed by the family members of the judge and police officers. One of the first things I did when I became Mayor was to terminate the contract with the city attorney and demand that the town Clerk return the business records and property of the town from his private office at a local farm. As a result of my action, I was again treated like a criminal for carrying out the job that I was elected to perform. The escapade continued when I discovered that the city government owned a facility that I was not allowed to use for official town meetings and only white residents of the community were permitted to use the facility. My demand that all citizens be allowed to use the facility was met with animosity and acrimonious accusations against me to prevent my success as Mayor of Glendora. I also discovered that the city's taxes had been tampered with that placed the town on a downward spiral towards financial devastation. It was difficult trying to reconstruct the financial system for the town of Glendora and I am sure some of the stolen or misplaced funds were never recovered.

My involvement in the political process was difficult for me. Politics were cruel and at times I was attacked by both whites and blacks. Whites did not want to see blacks break up the white power structure and some blacks were brainwashed by whites to think that having a black man in office would place their livelihood and the status of the town in jeopardy. After all, many of the black folks were employed by whites on their plantations, homes, and businesses, and had grown dependent on them for a livelihood. Many blacks did not vote, even after they had earned the right to do so, because they feared loss of their jobs or special privileges, especially if they voted for a black who was brave or "crazy" enough to pursue an elected office in Glendora or Tallahatchie County. The political process was tough for me because I was outspoken about community issues, always ran without compromising my integrity, and was willing to express my political views. Consequently, many whites labeled me as a radical. I was accused of arson several times, and of being involved in the murder of a town clerk. No matter how transparent I tried to be, some black people labeled me a sell-out, if I did not rule in their favor or made decisions that caused a hardship for them with their white bosses. I was knocked down many times, but I was never knocked out because I was always able to get back up and fight another round for what I believed in.

My Connection to the Emmett Till Case
"The Sins of Our Fathers"

Although many black families tried to shield their children from the vicious, emotional trauma that came with discovering or knowing about the brutal murders of black people in the area, sooner or later they heard talk or read stories about these killings that were all too common, especially in Mississippi and other parts of the South. I heard about the murder of Emmett Till at a young age from folks in the community who were talking about the mysteries surrounding the murder and the trial, including who was involved in the crime, the injustices involved in the trial of the two white men and the conspiracy, and the brutal way in which the murder was committed. Some of the people were around during that time or had family members or relatives who remembered the Till murder and trial.

The murder of Emmett Till continued to haunt the people of Glendora fifty years after this tragic event took place. An article in the newspaper asked, "Could blacks have participated in the murder of Till?" An internet blog that appeared on July 31, 2005 posed the following question: "Were blacks involved in the death of Emmett Till?" One of the blacks that the blog was referring to was my father, Henry Lee Loggins, who was working for J.W. Milam at the time that Emmet Till was murdered by Milam and Roy Bryant. When I was 11 or 12 years old, I heard some people in the community say that they believed my father was present at the murder of Emmett Till, and that he was arrested and whisked out of town to prevent him from telling what he knew about the murder or from later testifying at the trial. It was alleged by people in the area that J.W. Milam, forced my father to participate in the abduction and murder of Emmett Till.

Everyone knew that my father was one of the "right hand" workmen of J.W. Milam, who later confessed to the murder of Emmett Till, and it was rumored that Milam forced him to participate in the Emmet Till kidnapping and possibly the murder, and help dump Till's body in the Black Bayou to destroy evidence of the crime. I believe that my father was involved in the Emmett Till murder, was there with Milam and Bryant, and knew what was going on. However, out of fear for his life he did not admit to taking part in the crime or witnessing the crime. It was said that Till was shot through the head, and it was rumored that they took a drill and drilled a hole through his head; however, this was disputed by family members. Shortly after Emmett Till was murdered, my father was arrested by Sheriff Strider and secretly hidden in jail in nearby Charleston, Mississippi to prevent him from testifying and was later banished out of town to an unknown location. I heard that my father was jailed on a trumped-up charge that he stole some iron from Milam. Leroy

"Too Tight" Collins, one of Milam's workers, was also locked up in jail after the murder of Till.

J.W. Milam was the manager of several plantations in the area and serviced and maintained their farm equipment. Milam was a sort of plantation overseer whose job was to manage and control the black laborers who worked on the plantations in the surrounding area. Milam was a vicious, ruthless, roughneck, who did the dirty work in keeping black workers in their place for the plantation owners in Tallahatchie County. Milam was feared by black people and even some white people, and kept black people under control by beating them and threatening to kill them if "they had to be killed." I have been told by several people that they saw Milam actually beat black men to keep them in line or because they owed him money. He demanded total submission and obedience from his black workers, who feared his power and tyranny. Milam had been known to threaten to kill a black man, and his workers believed that he would actually kill them if they crossed him. My mother had a run-in with Milam when she was a field hand on the Flautts plantation. Milam beat my mother in front of her children because she refused to go to the fields to work because she was sick.

A resident of Glendora told me that Milam once ordered one of his men to wreck his truck by running it into a train so that he could collect the insurance money to purchase another vehicle that he liked. This man followed Milam's orders and risked his life by ramming Milam's truck into a train. Milam had the power and control to make his employees do anything he wanted them to do, even commit crimes or violent acts, because their livelihood depended on him and they were conditioned to obey their boss just like in the days of slavery when enslaved subjects were forced to obey their owner. This was a part of the culture that created fear, violence, and oppression that was perpetuated by the slave codes in the plantation system, and continued under the Jim Crow customs during the post-bellum period.

My father was vulnerable to this system because he had no power to change these conditions. Unfortunately, my father was a big womanizer, who borrowed money from Milam and was therefore indebted to Milam. Black children were socialized to fear Milam and other white people which created and perpetuated a culture of fear that was a form of oppression of blacks who lived in the area. Blacks did not fight back because their very livelihood depended on white people. Thus, black and white people were mutually dependent on each other that was enforced by a vicious cycle of fear, violence and oppression. Whites simply had no respect for blacks and their families, which was the same custom that existed more than 100 years earlier in 1857 when the U.S. Supreme Court ruled in the Dred Scott Decision that the black man had no rights that the white man had to respect.

Emmett Till's murder was definitely not the first time a black person had been murdered by a white person in Mississippi, in the South, or in the country. Three months before Till was murdered, Reverend George Lee, a grocery store owner and NAACP field worker was shot and killed in Belzoni, Mississippi, and Lamar Smith, another black man, was shot and killed in front of the county courthouse, in broad daylight and before witnesses, after casting his ballot. The internet estimated that during the Jim Crow era, approximately 1,500 blacks were murdered by whites in the U.S. and many other killings were unknown or unresolved, as to who did the killing.

According to Harvard Law Professor, Charles Ogletree, the murder of Emmet Till was unique in several ways from the other killings. The Emmett Till murder created outrage that two white men could kill only a child, even a black child, in such a brutal and horrific manner. Till was only 14 when he was murdered because he violated one of the cultural norms of the land—a black male whistled a white woman. Ogletree also believed that Till was killed to set an example for other blacks so that they would not dare to repeat this transgression, and to keep the black people of the area locked in fear so that they would be faithful servants to white people (Charles Ogletree, Interview, Harvard Civil Rights Project, *The Impact of the Emmett Till Case in American History*, 2005). Till was also killed to set an example for other blacks so that they would not dare to repeat this transgression, and to keep the black people of the area locked in fear so that they would be faithful servants to white people. Based on Jim Crow customs, Emmett Till had gotten "out of his place" and for this transgression, he was brutally killed. So, it was not just what these two white killers did to Till by destroying his body that was so despicable and shameful, to say the least, but it was what it did to attempt to keep other blacks locked in a state of fear so that they could continue to be exploited and so that white supremacy could continue to prevail.

Ogletree also pointed out that Till's murder was "unique" in that it occurred at a time when a national movement for civil rights was emerging across the country (Charles Ogletree, Interview, Harvard Civil Rights Project, *The Impact of the Emmett Till Case in American History, 2005*). Mrs. Rosa Parks sparked a movement of black resistance to segregation when she refused to move from her seat in the white section of the bus that was reserved for whites only in Montgomery, Alabama on December 1, 1955. Mrs. Parks stated that images of Till's murder crossed her mind when she refused to move to the black section of the bus or stand to let a white man sit down. Her behavior made a statement to the nation and the world that black people were willing to fight and suffer to gain their civil rights in a country that was still largely racially segregated, that was similar to the racial apartheid system in South Africa.

Not to be omitted is the fact that Emmett grew up in the North (Chicago). Blacks from the North were particularly despised by whites in the South because they were perceived as "trouble makers" or a threat to the welfare of the white kingdom. Northern blacks wanted to share in the wealth of the white kingdom. In particular, they wanted equality of education, employment, voting rights, political participation, and all human and civil rights that the majority of the members of the white kingdom was not willing to share, which was the main reason for the Civil Rights Movement. Professor Ogletree also pointed out that white people were more tolerant of black people in the North, where blacks could find more opportunities to improve their quality of life, compared to rural Mississippi or the South. For many blacks, the North was seen as a type of promise land here on earth where they could find more peace and happiness before they moved on to heaven (Charles Ogletree, Interview, Harvard Civil Rights Project, *The Impact of the Emmett Till Case in American History, 2005*).

The massive exodus of blacks out of the South and their migration to the North was a search for freedom, justice, and equality, at least more than they had in the plantation dominated economy of the

South. Thus, after the Civil War, a multitude of blacks left the South to seek their fortune primarily in the urban areas and cities of the North. Mrs. Mobley, Emmet Till's mother, was one of the people who left relatives in Mississippi in 1950 and established her residence on the south side of Chicago. In a sense, Till's visit to rural Mississippi to visit his kinfolk created the circumstances that led to a clash of two cultures between whites from rural Mississippi in the South and blacks from urban Chicago and other cities in the North (Charles Ogletree, Interview, Harvard Civil Rights Project, *The Impact of the Emmett Till Case in American History, 2005*). Mrs. Mobley did not know that the conditions were set for a horrific murder that was ignited by a playful act of a child, who whistled at a white woman, the wife of one of the men who murdered him for getting out of his place and crossing the racial line that violated a racial custom in Mississippi and the South.

How far would white men go to maintain a system of Jim Crow that was designed to protect the white kingdom of privileges, wealth, and power and the subjugation of blacks to white power so that they could be effectively exploited to create wealth for the white kingdom? The murder of Emmett Till indicated that members of the white kingdom were willing to go to extreme measures to protect their interests and gains, which they had built with enslaved or subjugated African people, including murders, lynchings, whippings, hangings, and other forms of brutal punishment. Black males were the main targets of the most brutal physical forms of white oppression because they were perceived as the greatest threat to the welfare of the white kingdom than were black women or children. It is a known fact that the vast majority of the victims of hangings, lynchings, and murders were black males. Although Till was only a 14-year-old- boy, he was the black male image of a threat to white power and rule. In essence, Emmett Till was murdered because he was a black male from Chicago who was fearless or "disrespectful" of white power, authority, and Jim Crow customs and was willing to die for it, and because he crossed the path of two racist white men who had been indoctrinated and acculturated with the doctrine of white supremacy, who were intent on keeping the white supremacy kingdom intact so that it could continue to promote the welfare of its members and constituents.

But the white kingdom was established in America, a country that claimed that "all men are created equal and that they are endowed by their creator with certain inalienable rights, that among them are life, liberty, and the pursuit of happiness." But in the case of African Americans, history has taught us that rights and privileges are not given; they must be earned at great cost through struggle and often in the face of resistance and violence, as experienced by Fannie Lou Hamer, from Ruleville, Mississippi, Rosa Park, Martin Luther King, Jr., and other civil rights leaders. Although Hamer said she was "sick and tired of being sick and tired," she continued her fight for the right to vote. By refusing to give up her seat on the bus to a white man, Rosa Parks made a statement that she was willing to fight for her human, civil, and constitutional rights, and that black Americans would fight to be covered under the Constitution of the United States of America. As such, this was the beginning of the bus boycott in Montgomery, Alabama and a major impetus to the Civil Rights Movement that was led by Dr. Martin Luther King, Jr. The Civil Rights Movement to gain human rights and end human wrongs was a long time coming but finally arrived. Thanks to all of the brave protesters who risked their lives and health to foster the cause of the movement.

For me, the most unique, personal, and intriguing aspect of the Emmet Till murder and trial is that they were located in the area where I grew up. My family knew people from Emmett Till's family and our fore relatives played together as kids—fished, hunted, and worked together. Till's body was dumped right here in the Black Bayou that runs into the Tallahatchie River, in the town of Glendora where my family lived. But most alarming is that my father, Henry Loggins, was the right-hand laborer of J.W. Milam, the white man who was tried for the murder of Till and later confessed to killing Till, along with his boss and half-brother, Roy Bryant. As a boy and young man, I heard rumors that my father was involved with the murder of Emmett Till. The day after Till was murdered, my father suspiciously disappeared from the area never to be seen again in Glendora until after the trial, when he sneaked into town to visit his relatives, which was the first time as an adult that I had seen him. There was still an element of fear, guilt, and shame among many blacks in the area who did not speak out against the murder of Till and other blacks in the area. They had become fixated by a culture of fear.

But on one occasion at the trial of Bryant and Milam, fear vanished when Moses Wright, Till's great uncle, stood up in the courtroom in Sumner where the trial was being held, and identified the two white men who abducted Till from his home in the early morning before he was murdered. This was the first time that a black man had testified against a white man in court in the history of Mississippi, and "lived to tell about it." This occurred in 1955 in Sumner, Mississippi. Perhaps a new day was dawning in Mississippi where there was a breakthrough in the culture of fear, intimidation, and racial oppression.

Years after the murder of Till, I became a marked man, labeled as the son of a black man named Henry Loggins, who possibly helped kill Emmett Till. This label and the mysteries that surrounded it have haunted me all of my life as I sought to raise my family in Glendora, even after I became Mayor and attempted to improve the social and economic conditions of the community. For more than 50 years, I have carried the burden that my father may have been involved in the Emmett Till murder. Although my father said that he had nothing to do with the murder of Emmett Till, I believe that he knew more than what he told us. I believe that out of fear for his life, he chose not to tell what he knew about the conspiracy and murder of Emmet Till. In 2005, when the Emmett Till case was reopened, I tried to get immunity from prosecution for my father if he would tell what he knew about the murder, but he insisted that he was not with them when they murdered Emmett Till. My father died in 2008 and took whatever information he might have known about the Emmet Till murder to his grave. He died in Dayton, Ohio in 2008 and with his death went possibly a critical piece of information surrounding the mystery of the murder of Emmett Till and the conspiracy that followed the murder. I conducted the last interview that my father gave.

How tragic it was that a 14-year-old child was brutally murdered by two white men for simply whistling at a white woman. It was also tragic that an all-white jury acquitted two white men for the murder of a young black boy, who later confessed to the murder, and that fear, racism, and disrespect for humanity, perpetuated by Jim Crow laws and customs, were so ingrained in the culture of the South that two white men could get away with murdering a child. Many people believed that Milam's and Bryant's confession was untruthful, and that they intentionally lied or twisted the truth to protect others who may have been involved in the murder. They also believed that some of the blacks knew more than what they told about the Emmett Till murder, but refused to tell out of fear for their life or job. Although racial oppression has significantly declined since 1955, there are still vestiges of fear of whites by blacks that are manifested in conscious and subconscious ways. There can be no real freedom, justice, and equality as long as there is a spirit of fear of whites by blacks.

Mayor Johnny B. Thomas' Words of Wisdom

These proverbs, words of truth and wisdom, and testimonies are expressions from Mayor Johnny B. Thomas, based on lessons learned from his life experiences in Glendora, Tallahatchie County, Mississippi.

- There are consequences for being first that are not always good.
- Never fear being first.
- When you fight for justice for yourself, you also help create justice for others.
- Always be ready to stand up for justice.
- Speak truth without fear!
- Conditioned ignorance breeds fear and poverty.
- You may not be the first to invent the wheel, but you can be first to speak truth and stand up for righteousness.
- Silence is sometimes betrayal.
- We are obligated to seek truth, speak truth, stand on truth, and stay with the truth.
- We must defeat poverty.
- Never sell your soul. There is a price to pay for telling the truth, and a greater price to pay for not telling the truth.
- To be a leader you will have some bright days and many dark nights.
- Be vigilant of your past or it will surely revisit you.
- You should never wait on the future to benefit you, you must fight for it now.

- You must be that stone of hope that Dr. King talked about in his "I Have a Dream Speech."
- No matter how much you fight for righteousness, prejudice will always be present.
- You must never be afraid to speak up for human rights or against human wrongs.
- Your dark past is on your heels; don't let it catch you.
- Never settle for instant gratification.
- As a stone of hope you are not easily broken.
- Nothing is more gratifying than standing up for others.
- You must fill the shoes of Emmett Till and continue the journey for justice.
- Begin your transformation, NOW!
- Always be ready to stand up for justice and speak out for justice without fear.
- Poverty begins with fear that one cannot rise above their present circumstances.
- Do not allow instant gratification and self-satisfaction to define your present or limit your future.
- The beginning of your journey for justice begins with your personal transformation.
- Don't let the sins of your father limit your present or define your future.
- If a person sees wrong and does nothing to correct it, he is guilty of the sin of omission.
- Slavery and the conditions that it supported and perpetuated were the sins of our fathers.
- If the spirit of a person is controlled by someone else, voluntarily or by force, he is defeated.
- Conditioned ignorance was characterized by whites with a false sense of superiority and blacks with a false sense of inferiority.
- One person's poverty can contribute to another person's wealth.
- People are still benefitting today because of the past sins of their fore parents.
- One of the most courageous acts that one can make is to own up to a painful truth of the past.

CHAPTER 8

MATRIARCHS AND PATRIARCHS

THE MATRIARCHS AND patriarchs of Glendora were pioneers who made significant contributions to the development of the town and community of Glendora. One matriarch was Elizabeth Hilson, who, along with her husband, Robert Hilson, built the first multi-purpose business complex that included an apartment, restaurant, auto mechanic shop, and a blacksmith shop. He and his wife were mentors to Willie James Stewart, who taught me much about how to operate a business and become self-employed.

During the early days, all African American babies born in the community were delivered by one of the African American midwives in the area. Mrs. Hester Stevenson was a local midwife who delivered babies in the area. She delivered me and all of my siblings. This was an important service because at that time, black people could not have their babies in the hospital, and if they could, they were not able to afford it. Mrs. Stevenson was like a mother to the whole community. She told me that she had seen one of the men who murdered Emmett Till beat other people in his store and was very frightened after Emmett Till was murdered, but had the courage to name one of her sons Emmett in honor of the slain 14-year-old Emmett Till. Other midwives who served the community were

Mrs. Francis Sims, Mrs. Mamie McKinley, and Mrs. Thelma White. These women provided the prenatal care for families in Glendora and Tallahatchie and also provided medical care for plantation workers and their families.

Four teachers who lived in the Glendora community at that time were Mrs. Henrietta Walker, Mrs. Jesse Williams, Mrs. Rosie Watkins, and Mr. Fred Watson. These teachers taught the African American children in the public schools, including those located on plantations in the county. They also taught the parents of the children.

Lauree and Willie James Stewart were highly respected residents of Glendora, who owned a barber shop business. Willie James was a mentor to me and other people in Glendora who aspired to own and operate their business. The businesses that they developed provided services to the community and also significantly contributed to the development of Glendora, especially during the 1960s and 1970s.

Mrs. Lillian Mitchell was the first African American to operate a racially integrated restaurant in Glendora during the 1970s, who provided a business model for women. Prior to opening her restaurant, she was a cook and domestic household worker for white families. Both black and white patrons were frequent customers at her restaurant, including Jewish merchants of the town and the surrounding area. Her hamburgers and stew were second to none. Her success story in rising from a domestic worker for white families to a business woman was an inspiration to many people in the area.

Although somewhat unusual in the black community, one matriarch was a white woman named Martha Lowe, who was the daughter of a prominent doctor and owner of Whitehead plantation, one of the oldest plantations in the area. The Lowe family provided finances to help black farmers start their farms in the Sharkey Road and Hampton Lake communities. They did a lot to help black families in Glendora, in spite of the fact that they were former plantation owners. One could say that her help to black families was a type of reparation or philanthropy to black families and their descendants, whose labor helped to generate wealth for white families.

Interview of Florida B. Smith
Sharkey Road, Rural Glendora

Thomas Durant (Interviewer): What is your name?

F.S. My name is Florida B. Smith. I was born in 1927 on the 14th day of January. That makes me 90, if you got your math right. I was born in Slaughter, Mississippi. Moved from there to a place they called High Point, out from Charleston, Mississippi. From there over to here on Sharkey Road. Where I was living at they call it Dirty Corner. Now I don't know why they called it Dirty Corner back in those days. Now they call it UPS Road. My mother and father were Mary and Calvin Spearman.

T.D. What was it like growing up in this area?

F.S. I had five step brothers and nine other sisters and brothers. There were 13 of us living at one time in the same house and we would have one chicken to feed all 13 of us. I wondered how in the world could she [mother] have enough to go around since a chicken has only nine pieces. But everyone would have a piece of chicken; some had a leg, a neck, liver. And she would have bread and potatoes and that's all. But everybody got full and everybody was healthy.

I first went to school at Mount Pleasant, on Sharkey Road. My first teacher was Miss Marlean. Our school was a one–room school in a church. We had to walk to school, three to four miles, and some places were farther than that. We had to be in school at nine o'clock. When you get there a lot of times you had to make a fire in the heater. At that time, they didn't have tin stoves, they had cast iron stoves they call them pot-belly stoves. A lot of times the parents and the men would cut wood and haul it to the school and the big boys would cut it up for firewood. A lot of times there wouldn't be no fire. We had to pick up trash and make a fire. Around the heater we had benches, wasn't no chairs. I remember the first book I had was Run Dan Run.

At recess time, the girls played on one side and the boys played on the other side. There was no such thing as lunches. You took your sausage and biscuit in a little jelly bucket. You carried your lunch in that. That's what we ate at recess time. At that time, school would start along about the middle of November. It would be out in March, because the big boys would have to go to the fields and work, you know. So, we just had a four-month school. I remember well, we were living at Charleston when we started with the nine-month school. People didn't know nothing about a bathroom. They had the outdoor toilets. Well now, they called it grass sacks, but we called it croaker sacks back then. The croaker sacks would be hanging up to it for the door.

Believe me, people back in those days raised what they needed— sweet potatoes, corn, and other crops. I remember stripping sorghum to make molasses. Mama 'nem raised chickens, ducks, geese, we raised all that stuff. And the men in the spring time, the men and the big boys, would have wagons and mules and go out and take the manure out of the barns and scatter it across the fields. Well, you know, that's the way they raised crops at that time. You know people weren't sick then like they are today. You never heard of people getting cancer like they do now. The children now go to the doctor and dentist, but they didn't do that when I was coming up. If a tooth got loosen, mama would put a string around it and snatch it out or take her hand and pull it out. We have come a long way.

When children would have fever, they would go in the hog lot and get a weed called Judson weed. They get the leaves off that and put around the child's head, or get some peach tree leaves and put around their head and break the fever. You know, there was not any doctors then to go to. Doctors were on call. At that time, they would come out, you didn't go to no doctor's office; they would come out to you. I would tell my children about the little smoothing irons and how we use to wash on the wash board. Back then gasoline wasn't but 25 cents a gallon. Other gas was like 20 cents a gallon. I remember Stacy Adams shoes that men wear, you could get for five dollars. You could get a bag of sugar for 25 or 30 cents.

I got corns on my hands from washing clothes on the wash board. And we had to iron our clothes using charcoals. We knew nothing about an electric iron or electric fan. Times have really changed. And my people living over there on Dirty Corner, I remember my daddy, he walked about nine miles to take a cow and calf. They [whites] would let you raise hogs and cows [on the plantation], but if you moved they would take them. I remember when daddy walked from Dirty Corner plumb over to Webb on Goocounter plantation with a cow and a calf about nine miles cause he was going to move. So by the time the white folks got there to get them, he was already gone. The white man came to the house later and asked my daddy where was the calf and cow and daddy said I don't know; the last time I saw them they were in the field. He lied. Daddy had taken the cows over to where he was moving to. We were living on the Reynolds place. After my dad moved from over there, he moved to Charleston and started renting. We stayed over there for two years.

My step daddy was a teacher. He was getting $60 a month. That's what they were paying them. He had to walk to school. I went to the 9th grade in school. You knowed as much in 9th grade as children do now with four years of college. Back then children could tell time by a clock with hands, but now children can only tell time by a digital clock. A friend of mine who is now 93, started teaching school when she was in the sixth grade, but she was still going to school.

T.D. What do you remember about sharecropping?

F.S. My father was a sharecropper. We lived in a four-room house that was owned by the plantation owner. We didn't pay no rent, just worked on the place. We were their niggers. If you worked on a plantation, your name was whatever it was, but you were known by the name of the owner of the plantation. Like there were Mr. Reynolds workers. Ollie Spearman became Ollie Cain because he was on the Cain plantation. My last husband was Daniel Smith, but he was known as Daniel Smith Mannings. It was almost like slavery time.

Coming up to Saturday and Sunday you would go to the commissary to get some fatback and other food and supplies. I remember when papa went there and got one bar of soap, one piece of fatback, and a little flour. Back during those times we would pick wild berries and pepper grass. We canned a lot of fruit and berries. But everything was owned by the white man. There was no credit, you just got a certain portion from the commissary. They kept the records. We didn't have no say so about nothing. If they got too far, they whipped the men. I don't remember them whipping the women. But I remember Mr. Mack told daddy he wanted the boys to burn stumps to make some new ground. Mr. Mack rode up on his horse and said to my dad, Sammy. He said, Yes Sir. He asked dad, Why aint Mary out there burning stumps? My dad said, Let me tell you something Mr. Mack. I married her, you didn't. So, she do what I say do. She aint burning no stumps. He said another word and papa rushed and got that hammer, and that man rode off and he never came back no more. But the next year we moved. We moved out of Charleston. One more man I heard tell of was B.J. Goss. A white man rode up and told him he wanted his wife to go to the field, so he told him that my wife didn't make no contract with you, I did. So she aint going to the field. I remember when women would put their babies on the porch and go to work. But things have changed now. But your president [Trump] want to take us back, but we aint going back here.

They made 40 bales of cotton one year and we cleared $500 dollars out of 40 bales of cotton. Twenty bales went to the white man and the other 20 bales went to us. But all of the expenses came out of our share, and nothing came out of the plantation owner's share. But a lot of people didn't get anything. I remember that when my daddy died my mother was living over there out from Charleston on a white man's plantation. And a white woman came out there from Charleston and told my mama, "Well Mary, you come out in the clear, you got a clear receipt." So, mama looked at her and told her that I can't do no more with a clear receipt than I can with a balance due. You know, back then you would go to the fields and work all day. It was no go to work at six and get off at seven. You go from sun to sun.

I picked cotton, hoed/chopped cotton, after I got old enough. I was about seven years old when I started picking cotton. My mother told me that if I picked 50 pounds of cotton, she would give me a stick of candy. So I did, I picked that 50 pounds of cotton and the next day if I didn't pick fifty pounds, I got a cotton stalk on my rear end. From then on I ended up picking 400 pounds of cotton before I quit picking. I knew of children who picked 200 to 300 pounds of cotton [a day].

We had midwives to help deliver babies on the plantation. Most people used midwives. Doctors would have to come out to the plantation sometimes and treat sick people, cows, and horses. All the doctors that I know were white doctors, who sometimes delivered black babies. My mother's last baby was born right over there on Dirty Corner and Dr. Freeman [a white doctor] came out to deliver the baby. Sometimes they would take women who could not deliver their baby to the hospital to have a C-Section. I saw one time they laid a woman across the bed and to get the baby out he had to put his foot against the bed to get the baby out, who was three months behind [overdue].

T.D. Did you ever hear of lynchings in this area?

F.S. I know some people got killed, but I don't know who killed them. I know they whipped them because they whipped a black man. But wouldn't no one white man go up to a black man and try to whip him. It would be four or five of them.

T.D. Were they afraid of black men?

F.S. They still are. One white man would never try to beat one black man then and you aint gonna get that now.

T.D. Why did they have such a fear of blacks when they had all of the guns?

F.S. I don't know. Black folks will fight because they always had to fight. Now they gone crazy fighting.

T.D. Why do you think white people could keep black people down for so long?

F.S. Sin and ignorance. They didn't know; they didn't have no education; that's all they know. Every now and then somebody like Martin Luther King will come up and deal with this situation.

T.D. Do you know of people who just got tired of the oppression and went out on Highway 49 and caught a ride out of here?

F.S. Yes, I know some people from over there in Tippo. They left because they had joined the NAACP. So when the white folks found out they had to leave. They went to Indianapolis, Indiana. They wanted to be free. They wanted to do better for themselves. Why do you think I am holding on to this little bit of land here. I am not going to sell it to the white folks. I worked too hard for this—62 acres. A lot of them have sold out, but I am still holding on. I told my children that when I am gone, you can rent it, but never sell it. I told my kids this. Don't never sell it.

T.D. If you had a chance to leave during that time, would you have left?

F.S. During that time, I would have left if I had the opportunity.

T.D. Tell me about your children.

F.S. I started my family when I was 18 years old. I have five girls and two boys living. One boy stays right down the road. The baby boy lives in Memphis. I got two girls in Memphis and three girls in Chicago. My oldest boy is 73. I knew Johnny's mama. I know when he was born.

T.D. Have all of your children been successful?

F.S. You see on that wall up there. Look on the wall. All of them graduated from high school and some graduated from college. One of my daughters taught school up there in Clarksdale; one is in Natchez and runs a daycare center. The next boy finished college. That girl there works for First Tennessee in Memphis. This one doesn't work nowhere. The baby girl of mine is a bank manager in Memphis. This boy right here is the janitor right there at the school.

T.D. What do you attribute their success to?

F.S. Education and working.

T.D. What was the most memorable thing you remember about growing up in Tallahatchie County, Mississippi?

F.S. I remember that I never wanted to work for no white folks. When I was a little girl, I saw how they did my mama. She use to wash for them and they would give her a jar of molasses and maybe three dollars. I always wanted to be something like a secretary. I helped my dad when he got ready to make a loan for his farm stuff. I would go with him and learn how to do business. He would tell me what to put on the papers and I would write it up. He would ask me to write out how much to order in goods and supplies like beans and meat. We would go to the bank and borrow the money to buy the stuff. That's how I learned what to do. But he died and mama was ready to let the place go, but the banker said I will help you all out. Dad was 51 when he passed. Mama was about 69 when she passed. I was five years old when my stepdad died. My mother was married four times and she got a child by each husband. She never had but four children. A lot of people had common law marriages and some got a license. A license cost about three dollars.

T.D. What message would you give to young people on how to live today?

F.S. Be truthful, try to have a level head and pray to God for guidance cause you can't do nothing on your own. That's the main thing. Keep Christ in your life. The flesh is never going to want to act right. I always taught my children. I aint going to tell no lie, I did things I shouldn't have did cause I was not gonna let my children go hungry or barefooted. I never stole nothing. I always tell my children, you don't have to steal and don't lie to get nothing. I told them now if you go out there and somebody is picking on you and you get in a fight, you got to protect yourself, and if you go to jail you can call me. But if you get in jail for stealing something, don't call me cause I aint coming. Cause you don't have to steal. I had two of my boys locked up. The one that died, I had gone to church and my husband was going to take a bath so he laid his billfold on the shelf. And when he came out of the bathroom he didn't see it. So when I came I asked him did you move your dad's billfold. He said no I aint got it. So, I said it was only you and him here and the billfold aint got no legs. So I questioned him about it again and he still lied, so I called the police. He was the police down there in Glendora named Big Mack. He called me and said what do you want to do with him. I said put him in a cell and throw the key away. My husband had a fit.

He started walking the floor. He wanted to get the boy out and said only $30 was in the wallet.

The boy who is a janitor was going to burn the house down because he was mad. So, I called the police on him and had him locked up. So, the girls came here from Memphis and said can we get him out and I said you can get him out but he aint coming back here. You can't pay him today to take anything from my house. I done tried it. I would drop a $5 bill in the bathroom or somewhere. He would tell me that you dropped some money. I tried him to see if he would do it. Because they know that I told them I don't have any money for no white folks. I aint paying out no money to them for you. I aint gonna do it. Sho' aint. They don't have to do that. And I tell these young folks. My little grandson, I tell him now look, you curse your mama out, you don't want to go to school to get your education, so, I said when your mama put you out, don't come here. I got a stick over there and I said I will beat your brains out boy. I say no, no don't come this way. I said there is plenty of work for you to do. Go out there and cut grass. Its something you can do to make your money earnestly. You don't have to go out there and steal. These young folks, if you let them, they will lay up on you and don't do nothing for themselves. My grandson can cook better than I can. Every child I got can cook except one who can't boil hot water or an egg, cause my mama kept him until he was 10 years old. He changes his own bed because I brought them up like that. I always kept my yard up. Now I would always give them a little something. I'm gonna try you to see if you will do anything without me telling you. Some kids you have to tell them everything. You have to tell some of them how to take a bath.

Interview of Christine V. Wheeler
Sharkey Road, Rural Glendora

What is your name?

My name is Christine V. Wheeler. I was born in 1938 in Leverett, Mississippi, Tallahatchie County. I grew up as a single child in the 1940s and 1950s. My mom and dad never lived on a plantation, but they lived in between two large plantations owned by Caucasians.

They rented land on a fourth plan from whites for farming. So I learned what plantation life was like. I would see people come and get folks out of bed to go and work on the plantation. I helped my daddy with farming. I operated the harrowing plow behind two mules. A Caucasian who saw me plowing stopped and did the plowing for me because he thought it was cruel for a young girl to be plowing. This was unheard of during that time. When I was only seven years old I could ride a horse and herd cows. I could shoot a gun and do all the things mostly that a boy could do. I also kept the house clean for mom, washing, ironing. All of us had to pick and chop cotton. It was a way of life then. No it wasn't good when you look at it from the outside, but when you live in a situation, you learn to deal with it.

I got into a lot of trouble when I was a young girl in Charleston because my grandfather, my mom's dad, was a logger. My mom and dad couldn't drive. So, one day I was sitting in the log truck and the truck started rolling, full of logs. I had watched grandpa drive and knew what to do and he had showed me how to stop the truck. After I stopped the truck, I drove it all the time after then. I was only about nine or ten years old. Once I drove around the courthouse the wrong way and they got after me, but they let me go because grandpa was well respected because his logging business was bringing money into the town. I got into trouble like that. I refused to call young Caucasian people mister or miss because you tell me that I have to call them mister or miss and they are only 12 years old, the same as me? I refused to do it, so I got in trouble like that. I didn't back off from nothing. A white man once told me that I wouldn't live to reach 20. He said that unless I was made to obey the rules, I would never make it to 20. But after he became a judge and my mother called me to come home from San Francisco to help them with some legal matters, he looked at me and said, you mean to tell me that you are still living, and still got a big mouth? I said listen, let me tell you something. You got the degree, but let me tell you what's going on. I said my mom and dad don't know how to talk for themselves so that's why I'm here. That's why I made it here. And that day I won the case for them. So, he say to me, You made it didn't you, and I said yes sir, I made it. And I still got the same attitude I had when you knew me back then. He said, you are here in the court and I let you have your way, and you win it for your mom and daddy.

T.D. Do you think that white men were more tolerant of black women than black men?

C.W. Yeah, they were, because even today, if white men like black women, black women could get away with things that black men couldn't.

T.D. Why do white men like black women?

C.W. I don't know, but it has been like this for years and years. I don't know why they like them. When I was a child, I saw kids were lighter than me and I thought that the daddy was their daddy, but he wasn't their daddy. One day we slipped off and went across the bridge to Swan Lake to go to the store. The man in the store filled our bags with good stuff and said get out of here quick. And I asked why was he so nice to us? He didn't even take our money. We talked about it all the way back home. Poor mother had been looking for us. Mama said you are not to go over there to that store. Let me tell you, don't ever do that again. I learned later that the white man at the store was my cousin's daddy. He had been going with her mother. We were children and didn't know. And mama say, look baby, there are some things that children are not supposed to know, but we told you all not to go over there to that store. He was kind of a heavy-set man. That's what happened.

T.D. What did black children say when children came out looking white?

C.W. They felt helpless to do anything about it. But they loved their children regardless. Most of the Caucasians have some black folks in their family. That's what happened then. And that's what happened all through slavery. The white men would take the black women and the white women would force the butler and black men who worked for them to go with them. All of this stuff has been going on for generations. So, I have to accept the situation that I'm in. I may not like it but I have to accept the situation that I'm in. So, that's what it was like at that time. And it is still happening today, but at least it is "if I want to." People have more freedom to marry or go with whomever they want to go with. Yes, the black woman get on the black man for marrying white women, when they get to be somebody. But if you are going to school with them every day this is what happens. And the Bible say love, it did not say who to love. So, we must accept that too. And when I came to realize that the Bible says love ye one another, not by race or creed, but love ye one another, the Bible does not look at color, but we have been down and mistreated so badly by Caucasians that we can't accept that. I have accepted it because I have a choice and I decided to love. My son-in-law did not like it. In slavery, blacks didn't have a choice. Now we have a choice to marry who you like. And that's alright with me. The sin back then is that you were made to do what you did not want to do. So, that was the sin in slavery and when my mom and daddy grew up.

T.D. You have been very successful in life. What is the reason for your success in life?

C.W. Even though I knew there was separation and that it was wrong, I never saw the color of a person. Someone told me that you don't act like you are black? I say why do you say that? They say, because you don't talk like blacks do, saying yes sir and no sir, and all this stuff. I say they are people just like me and we are around the same age. So, hey, when I left here and went to San Francisco I did hate. I hated because we had to go through so much.

T.D. You hated white people?

C.W. Yes, I hated some white people and I hated some black people too. No matter how smart you are, you still would come out on the losing end. They would get you when you buy or sell your crop. The price would go down for your crop but yet it would go up for the other man. I hated that bureaucratic system during slavery. I told a white banker, I know you drive a hard bargain, but you are not going to take that white man's place, but you will take that black man's place and sell it to a white person. He didn't like me for saying that. They starting foreclosing on daddy and that's why we had to sell some property to pay them off. And that became the norm. A white lawyer told me on his dying bed, I can show you the paper work of what I did to take the places and the property of blacks. This white man was dying with cancer when he admitted that he had been taking black folks' land. I knew something was wrong with my parents' deeds because there was one word in it that I couldn't pronounce or didn't know what it meant, but I knew that it was sitting in the wrong place. So I took a photo copy of it and took it to San Francisco to my lawyer. He say that if she died, they would take that place, and you wouldn't get a thing. And that's what happened to most of the people. They thought they had something and didn't. In another case, a man thought he owned his place. He died and they put his wife and children off the place because they said it was theirs. So, I came and took care of business for mom, because I had a lawyer who advised me what to do.

I progressed because I found Christ and I lost the hate. They sent me to a bank in San Francisco in a very affluent neighborhood. They didn't like me, but since I found Christ, I was loving and couldn't help it. And I said I love people and I can't help it. I worked at a bank in that neighborhood and people would walk up to my window and tell me no black person is going to take care of my business. I guarantee you that in less than a year and a half, those same people said that if you walk out of this bank they will have to close it because I will take my money out of it. They kept me right there. The millionaires looked after me and made sure I had a parking space. They took care of me. They kept me there. But you can't do it until you love. No, didn't all of them like me, but I treated them with kindness. I never cursed them. Before I left here I knew how to curse. I could say words to make you want to kill me. But I would look at them with a smile. My Husband wasn't quite like I was. But it was a good thing that he left because he might have been dead too. He was liked on the job he was on and the Lord just let us progress. But we were blessed because the Lord God took care of us and brought us back here. He died here.

T.D. What did you know about Dirty Corner?

C.W. People used to tell us that the James brothers had their riders and they would take them [blacks] back in Dirty Corner and they had something like a prison or stockade there. They would beat and kill black people and punish them, and hang them and stuff. And nobody did anything about it. That was before my time. It stayed Dirty Corner until they built some houses back there and named the road UPS. Today I can't watch movies about blacks being beaten and abused. I have to pray on that. You just can't do people like that and get by.

Right in this area was a huge plantation owned by the James brothers. There were different communities in this area. Dirty Corner was located in an isolated area where the James brothers would go and do their dirt. But they got into trouble with the federal government for not paying income taxes and the government seized their land along with that of several other large plantations. The federal government divided this land up into 60 and 80 acre parcels and sold the property to Negroes. That was in 1945 or 1946. It was the UFCA and the FHA who divided up the land. They also divided up the livestock. We own about 150 acres of land. The Caucasians did not want us here and they didn't like us. But we worked hard from early morning to late evening.

At that time, there were no black children in jail. The Emmett Till murder was a terrible situation. But let me tell you something. If the rivers, lakes, and bayous could talk, it would make Emmett Till look shame. They would kill a Negro man or boy for nothing and put him in the bayou. I had many cousins who were beat up and castrated. It was just evil. And then some white woman would tell a lie on a black man. That's what happened in the Emmett Till case. Some of the white women forced black men to go with them and said that if you don't, I am going to tell a lie on you and you gonna be dead just the same.

But over time things got a little better. Dr. King and other people marched and things got a little bit better. But back then you found people hanging in trees, killed, and for nothing and nothing was done about it. One doctor came in here from Orlando and set up a hospital to treat the people. He knew he had to wait on the white man first, and if he was working on a black person and a white person came in, he would have to stop working on the black person and work on them.

T.D. How was the church involved in the Civil Rights Movement in this area during the 1960s?

C.W. The church has always been a gathering place for black people. The church was a place where blacks could go and socialize. Mostly all of the large plantations would let the blacks have a church to worship on Sunday. The church was also a place where blacks could come to deal with the situations, conditions, and hardships that they were dealing with. Martin Luther King organized people through the church, which was a part of the Civil Rights Movement. Most of the people who were marching for their rights were from the churches. I take my hat off to the people who opened their homes to the marchers who came here to help with the demonstrations. They provided places for people to stay because there were no hotels in the community. They opened their homes up to strangers, blacks, whites, and people of all colors, to come here to help in the Civil Rights Movement. My mom was the first kindergarten teacher to bus black children to integrated schools. The church played a big part because when King came along he practiced non-violence, although some of the marchers got attacked and hurt. But the older people stood up. I am so proud when I think about my mom and dad helped feed the marchers who came down here. They said that they are coming here to help us and we are going to feed them. I could not be here, but I sent money to them to buy food to prepare for the marchers. At that time, the community was just full of people who came with Dr. Martin Luther King to help the community. The churches played a big part in this. It is not playing as big a role now as it did then because a lot of things have gotten better. And it is better. But I tell the young people today that even though you don't remember some of the things that went on during my life, it was rough. But if you are a black person you should know your history.

Interview of James Madyun
Rural Glendora

T.D What is your name?

J.M. I was born James Lofton, but I got a Muslim name by Elijah Mohammad when I came out of the Army, and I changed my name to James Madyun. I was born in Minter City, Mississippi in 1940.

My mama and my sister were from Minter City. I had two sisters and no brothers. My daddy was an only child and had three children by his first wife, nine by my mother, and three more on the side. He was a sharecropper, but at the end of the year he didn't owe anybody. The owner of the plantation where he sharecropped was named Mr. Clyde. I don't remember his last name. We called him Mr. Clyde. My mother and father came up here in 1950. We have 75 acres of farm land and 125 acres all together. This area was called Dirty Corner. I heard people tell stories, which I don't know if they were true or not, but I heard that they use to bring Negroes down here and lynch them. I don't know if that is true or not, but that is where the word Dirty Corner came from. If you put the name in the GPS, it will come up with the same place here, Dirty Corner. You can find the place on the GPS as Dirty Corner.

T.D. What were your experiences in sharecropping?

J.M. At the Ridge plantation they use to pay me 50 cents a head for every person I brought over there to chop cotton. All I had to do was sharpen the hoes and give them cold water. I made more money than they did just by bringing them over there. When we finished working on our farm we would go over there and make money like that. My mother told us to get some land and put a house on it. They call me old school. When we went to Charleston for the Martin Luther King parade not one white person was in the parade. Now that's arrogance.

T.D. Tell me what you know about the Civil Rights Movement that occurred in the 1950s and 1960s in this area.

J.M. I can't tell you the first names, but I can tell you the family names of some of those involved. My stepfather Jesse Thompson and my mother Ethel Thompson were involved. There were several families involved in this area. They communicated by CB radio. They used a tall tower for communication with each other by CB radio. They say Stokeley Carmichael came down here, who was leader of SNCC [Student Non-Violent Coordinating Committee]. The leader of CORE [Congress of Racial Equality] also came down here. But some of the black folks were afraid that the white people would get mad about that. CORE and SNCC were more radical than SCLC that Dr. King was over.

I sold newspapers from the Chicago Defender from Chicago, a black newspapers from Chicago. They would send them to me and I would sell them down here in the early 1980s. Mama stopped me from selling the newspapers down here because she was afraid that the white people would get mad if they found out about it. The white folks down here thought that the Chicago Defender would start a rebellion among the black people for civil rights. They wanted to hide information from blacks about their civil rights. They didn't want Negroes here to learn about their civil rights. But black people were going to survive.

T.D. Why do you think some blacks civil rights leaders were brave enough to speak out for their civil right?

J.M. They didn't give up. There is always a fighter somewhere. Somebody is always going to challenge the system. I was 15 years old when Emmett Till was murdered, just a year older than him. We were not afraid. My mother bought all of her boys a gun. She bought me a 22 rifle and I started carrying my gun in my truck. We said that if we were attacked, we were not going down without a fight. Some of us left here. But a lot of the teenagers were not afraid. We knew that they killed Emmett Till and I knew that although I was only 15 years old at the time that I was vulnerable too. I don't think Emmett Till whistled at her. This young man was sharp. He wore nice clothes. He was clean. I think the real problem was that these guys [whites] didn't like white women looking at black guys. When I saw the movie Mandingo it showed how this white man had him an African American maid, and had a baby by her. He was showing black people that I can have a black woman but you cannot have a white woman. That's the way it is when people have power they can do what they want to do.

T.D. Do you think that race relations will ever get better?

J.M. It gets better, then it gets worse. In North Carolina I heard that they got rid of all of the racists on the school board. If we did that all over, we could get rid of the racial problem. We have an all-white private school in this area; they may have one black student in order to get federal funds. Medgar Evers was a civil rights leader in this area and some of the civil rights organizations also helped, like CORE and SNCC. Most of the civil rights leaders around here were women. We had a few men leaders who spoke out like my stepfather, Jesse Thompson. I left here in 1957 and came back when I got out of the army. Most of the people around here came from the plantations in the area. The Catholic Charity helped build houses for people in this area. Danny Glover came down here and they say Bobby Kennedy also came down here around 1966. Every community has somebody strong like Fannie Lou Hamer in Ruleville. I spent 27 months overseas in the military in Germany. They had racial problems over there too. The white German girls refused to dance with the black soldiers but would dance with the white soldiers.

T.D. Why did you join the Muslims?

J.M. I met a woman in Chicago who told me that she was Muslim and they didn't vote. She said symbolically, we are Jesus because we are the ones being crucified and bearing the cross. Boy, that woke me up. I understood that as plain as day. They teach us not to fear man, but fear God. You are not supposed to fear man, you suppose to fear God. At one time they wouldn't let no white folks join.

Interview of Beatrice B. Smith
Retired Teacher
Glendora

Linda Taylor, Graduate Student, Jackson State University: What is your name?

B.S. My name is Beatrice B. Smith. I was born and reared in Glendora on Mr. T.C. Buford's plantation. I am 88 years old and was born on November 28, 1927. I have four children, two living and two deceased. My children also live here. My mother passed when I was a baby and my grandparents raised me. I was the baby of the bunch and they petted me all the time. I never got whippings like some children do.

L.T. What was life like growing up on the Buford plantation?

B.S. When I was growing up, I didn't know a whole lot about what was going on, but we were sharecroppers. We thought we were doing real good, but we didn't know we were poor. Everybody was in the same shape so we didn't know we were poor. We just did the same thing year in and year out, sharecropping on the plantation. As a young girl, I worked on the Buford plantation with my family who were sharecroppers. We didn't get very much. They would haul us to the field. We got lunch in the fields. One person would bring us water and one person would take our names. We chopped cotton and picked cotton. We had to tote our sacks and empty our sacks. We had to help other families who were not doing as well as we were doing. There was a woman who was pregnant and we had to go and help her family. My mother took care of all of the children of all of the people who were working in the field. She raised three sets of children until her health failed.

At that time, we didn't have a refrigeration and stuff like that. We would pick peas, sweet potatoes and other crops and put them in the cellar. We had a cellar. We had hogs, cows, and chickens. We raised sorghum and made molasses. The sorghum grinder was driven by a horse to get the juice to make the molasses. We had plenty of molasses to eat in the winter. On the weekend we would wash our clothes and iron them with a smoothing iron that was heated on coals. We got our water from the bayou. They taught the girls how to cook and the boys did the outside work. We made lye soap from hog lard, ashes, and water to wash our clothes with. The men killed rabbits and we got fish from the bayou. At one time, the county gave us some kind of commodities like cabbage, cheese and flour.

The landowner would send a doctor to us if we needed one. At the end of the year the owner would give us a little money. It never would be enough but they would give us a little money to make it through the winter. Now let me tell you about the cemetery. The plantation had a cemetery for us to be buried in. The owner also had a church built for us on the plantation. I was a member of the Methodist Church that the landowner had built for us. It was a nice little Methodist church when it was new. People would come from far and near to see this little Methodist church on the plantation. I was the Mistress of Ceremony at the church all of my life. I traveled across the United States doing missionary work. I still have my membership there. That's the only church I have ever been a member of.

L.T. When did you leave the Buford plantation?

B.S. I have been off the Buford plantation for about 50 years. I moved over to the government projects. They sold or rented the plantation. However, every year we used to have a Buford Day when everybody who lived on the Buford plantation would come out. Mr. Buford and his wife and their children would come out and celebrate with us. The old man is deceased but his son who was still living would come out.

L.T. Tell me about your education?

B.S. In our community, we had school in the church. The teacher lived on the same plantation with us. Her name was Mrs. Mabelle Hudson. Her mother was Adeline Coleman, who also was a school teacher. Our teacher was going to school to be trained at the same time she was teaching us. Sometimes we walked to the church school together and had to make a fire when we got there. A man who lived near the school started making a fire for us. We didn't have no car. One day I caught a ride with the plantation secretary who picked me up and took me to school. The teacher chose me to go to school to be a teacher along with a few others. We went to Greenwood where we were all in training to be teachers. Although we had not finished school ourselves, we did qualify to be teachers. When the principal chose me to go for teacher training I was pregnant. I told the teacher that I felt funny and I thought I was pregnant. I don't know why she laughed, but when she stopped laughing she said I don't want no one but you to go for the teacher training. I first started teaching the second grade. Then I left the second grade and started teaching the first grade. I was teaching Johnny B. and I had a large group of students. Some of the kids in the first grade were older kids but they knew a lot.

I was able to get my degree in elementary education from Mississippi Valley State University. It took me about six years because

I had to work while going to school. My family borrowed money from the plantation owner for me to go to college and we had to pay him back. I had to pick cotton to make money for school. Both of my sons went to Valley.

Now let me tell you about Johnny B. a little. He was one of my students. I saw that he was somewhat smart but they didn't send him to school like they should have. One day I was coming from work and he was on the roadway. So, I called him and he got off the roadway and came and asked me what I wanted. I told him I want to sponsor you in my adult education class so that you can get your high school diploma. I said it is going to cost you a little bit but I want you to do it. He did just like I told him. He had to take that test and I told him you can pass it, I know you can do it. And he passed the test and got his high school diploma and started working out here in Glendora. I worked with the school for 38 years and worked in adult education for 12 consecutive years.

Interview of Eddie James Meeks
County Supervisor & Former Judge
Tutwiler, Mississippi

T.D. What is your name?

E.M. My name is Eddie James Meeks. I am 60 years old. I am Supervisor for Tallahatchie County, District 5. I was born in 1957, two years after the Emmett Till murder.

T.D. What is your family background?

E.M. My father was Joe Willie Meeks. He lived in the Mississippi Delta almost all of his life in Tallahatchie County. He moved to Sunflower County, and then backed to Tallahatchie County, still working on the farm. He worked on the Rainbow Plantation. My mother was Irene Cohn Meeks. She mostly did household work on the farms where my father worked. She did some cotton chopping for about three dollars a day.

T.D. What was it like for your family being sharecroppers?

E.M. Sharecropping was pretty hard, but we never needed anything that we didn't get. We raised our food. My mother had 13 children. I am the seventh child. We raised all of our food. We raised cows, hogs, crops, and whatever we needed so we never went hungry. My mother used to have about a two-acre garden. We raised fruit, vegetables, okra, cucumbers, and things like that. We also had plenty of food stored up. We had fig trees. I don't ever remember being hungry. We didn't eat what I wanted to eat, but we always had food. At the end of the year when all of the sharecroppers settled up, I never remembered my family coming out to the point where we didn't owe anything. My father always had to borrow money for Christmas holidays and ended up paying it back later. They stayed in debt all year to pay back that five or six hundred dollars they borrowed for the Christmas holidays. Basically, all of the sharecroppers lived like that.

T.D. What was living on the Rainbow Plantation like?

E.M. Rainbow Plantation was a more liberated group of white people. They hired black kids and let them use their swimming pool to learn how to swim. The kids that had connections to Rainbow Plantation were the only ones that knew how to swim on the west side of Tallahatchie County. If I had to work on a plantation, the Rainbow Plantation is where I would have selected.

T.D. Did Rainbow Plantation have a commissary?

E.M. No. I lived on only one farm that had a commissary and that was Brooks Farm in Sunflower County. My father worked down there for about four or five months, but just couldn't take it. The closest we ever came to getting hungry was down there because my daddy didn't have a big garden spot and he wasn't making any money. And the commissary was so high if you bought anything there. So, my daddy and his family stayed there for three or four months and then moved back to the same farm [Rainbow Plantation] he had moved away from. And he got a small increase in salary.

T.D. How many years did your family sharecrop?

E.M. All of my life until 1975. My daddy stayed on until I could help build them a house. I didn't have any money to build the house but there was a teacher at the West Tallahatchie School District who had an old house that we tore down and used all of the bricks and lumber to build a house for my dad and his family. That was the first house that we owned and the first house built [by blacks] in Tallahatchie County. They stayed on the Rainbow Plantation up until 1997, about 20 years ago. He stayed there longer than I did because I went into the military in 1975 and got out in 1980. Then I met up with Johnny B. [Thomas] and them, and they introduced me to public office.

E.M. All of the 13 children moved off the Rainbow Plantation at different times except my sister who had Downs Syndrome and stayed with my father on the plantation.

T.D. Is the Rainbow Plantation still in operation?

E.M. No it is not. It is still being farmed but not by the Rainbow Plantation family. It is now a commercial farm.

T.D. Could you tell me about your schooling and education?

E.M. I graduated from West Tallahatchie High School in 1975. When I got out of high school, I married at the age of 18 and my wife was 17. We have been married for 41 years. I went in the military in June of 1976 and came out a littler earlier than June 1980 because I got credit for comp time. When I got out of the military, I met Johnny B., Jerome Little, Robert Huddleston, and guys that had stayed back here and they were a real inspiration to me because some of the things that I wanted to see done they were trying to do and they needed young black men to stand up and be counted. So, we formed this group [Magnificent Seven] and that's what we did. You might have had one or two black-elected officials in Tallahatchie County but it was mostly the ones that white people knew that anything they wanted them to do they would do. They knew that the white people controlled everything, even whether they could get elected again. Most of the time they were pretty fair to be, but Johnny B. was fighting and Jerome Little was fighting. Robert

Huddleston, L.D. Willis, Richard P. Gardner, Gyrone Kenniel and myself were all fighting. And we had Attorney Margaret Carey from the Center of Constitutional Rights helping us, who is now a Circuit Judge over in the Greenville area. She was our attorney. She came down and camped out in Tallahatchie County. Any black person that was elected in Tallahatchie County got Margaret Carey to help them because she camped out here and helped us with the redistricting. Also Victor Macter and Mike Sayers from the Southern Echo helped us and worked with us real stringently to help bring about changes in Tallahatchie County. You would have to know where Tallahatchie County came from to appreciate where we are now. Tallahatchie County is a whole lot better than it has been but it has been plagued by two things and that's racism and poverty.

The Free State of Tallahatchie, that's what we are called, is on the west side of the county. The east side of the county is majority white and pays less taxes than the west side of the county that is majority black and pay most of the taxes in the county but get less benefits. The Emmett Till courthouse is in Sumner, which is in Tallahatchie County. I wasn't a big advocate of the Emmett Till Courthouse museum project. I didn't want it to come to Tallahatchie County for reasons that I thought people were using Emmett Till and exploiting the Emmett Till situation. It wasn't about what happen to this young kid and what happened to his family and the struggles that they went through. It wasn't about that for the people that I saw that were still with Emmett Till. It was about Tallahatchie County getting a new courthouse and didn't have to spend county funds on it. They thought that Tallahatchie County could get this or get that if we could get the Emmett Till Courthouse to come here. I fought it all I could but Jerome Little and Johnny Thomas were part of our group who fought to get it here. They won out. But now I sit on the County Board of Supervisors and now understand why Jerome Little fought to get it and I'm going to do everything I can do to make sure that it lives up to what it is supposed to live up to. I'm not going to try to fight it. I see some disappointment in the way things happened. The Emmett Till Multipurpose Facility was located in an old factory building that was being renovated to be used for that purpose. However, the funding just got cut off because the only thing they seemed concerned about was the white areas. I didn't like the way that some of the white people, according to my understanding, were involved in the Emmett Till killing who owned some of the property around the courthouse and they sold it for an astronomical price when they found out that the courthouse was going to be made into the Emmett Till Courthouse. That was one of the reasons I was fighting it.

I went to Mississippi Valley State University while I was still working because I was married. My major was accounting and my minor was business administration. I got 38 credit hours before I quit because in the Delta, once you get married you have to take care of your family. I stayed at Mississippi Valley about a year and a half. I was still able to do some things, but I just wasn't in a position to stay in school. Then I turned around and went to Coahoma Community College. I took up carpentry and at one point I got my contractor's license, but my financial situation kept me from keeping my license because you had to buy insurance. Then the market crashed when President Obama came in. I stayed at Coahoma College about two years but I didn't get a diploma. So, things got hard and nobody wasn't doing any work.

T.D. You mentioned a group of people who stood up for their civil rights in Tallahatchie County. Were they a part of the Magnificent Seven that was involved in the Civil Rights Movement in Tallahatchie County?

E.M. Yes, they were. Johnny B. and Jerome Little, who had gotten out of the Marines, were doing things before I got out of the military. The first thing they did was to put me up to run for the School Board.

T.D. Why did you decide to run for public office?

E.M. The office I won was Election Commissioner. As Election Commissioner, I made Johnny Thomas the first black Supervisor in Tallahatchie County, but he never got a chance to take his seat. The first person that ever printed the ballot for Tallahatchie County other than the white Clerk of Court was me because I took my job seriously and was going to do all that I could do because they [whites] had been stealing ballots. We had people in Tippo who voted before the pools opened at 7:00 a.m. because their boss said they had to go to work about 60 miles away and had to be on time. They had white people who were running the polls then. They came in and stated that their people had to be at work and they opened the polls before 7:00 a.m. About 45 votes were cast before 7:00 a.m. These votes were illegally cast. We threw out the 45 votes from the Tippo box and that put Johnny B. over the top. We had warned them and told them that this would be a contested election and to open the polls on time but they decided that they would open the polls about an hour and fifteen minutes early. They took the case to the Mississippi Supreme Court, and the federal court, who kicked it back to the Supreme Court and all of this was done in less than a two-week period. But eventually a judge came to Tallahatchie and when he saw that the jury would not act he ruled not to overturn our decision to throw out the illegally cast votes. I do not remember the name of the judge.

You were the Election Commissioner when this happened?

E.M. Yes. I was Election Commissioner for four years. I was a justice court judge for eleven years. As Election Commissioner, I had qualified to run for judge but I had gotten kicked off because they waited until after the qualifying deadline and took my name off the ballot because the law stated that once an Election Commissioner run and win the office, he couldn't run for another office during the four years he held that office. I filed a law suit that went all the way to the Mississippi Supreme Court, Meeks vs Tallahatchie County. We got the ruling overturned but it didn't do me no good because the decision came too late. Ellis Turnage from Cleveland, Mississippi was my attorney who got the case to go to the Mississippi Supreme Court.

T.D. You mentioned that Tallahatchie has been plagued by racism and poverty. Could you explain a little more about that?

E.M. The racism is that it is hard to get black folks to vote because we don't have nothing to offer. They work on the farms and their [white] boss said don't catch the truck tomorrow if they voted for black people. We don't have jobs to give them. The farmers [whites] got mad with them if they voted for black people. Black folks don't own any businesses in Tallahatchie County and usually when most of these towns get taken over by blacks...I have not seen one town that was previously run by whites where blacks were able to fix the streets after blacks took over. It seems like the work stops and the money dries up. Even with the County it is the same thing. Tallahatchie County has a real serious problem with poverty and the Board of Supervisors still have a plantation mentality. On the last working day of the month, all of the laborers come to the court house and stand around like they are getting a free paycheck. They can't get a direct deposit. You have people that actually fight direct deposits. Progress is coming but it is real slow.

T.D. Why is there so much poverty in Tallahatchie County?

E.M. I'm just going to tell you straight up. A lot of these programs that come to Tallahatchie were not able to help Tallahatchie County. Take for example, the Jerome G. Little Manor housing complex in Sumner and other HUD properties that could have given two or three jobs each to people. But for some reason, somebody saw fit to let Tesco Properties, a white organization out of Memphis manage these properties and they have Mexicans to do most of the work. They also bring people from out of town. Out of all of those housing projects the regulations make it difficult to operate a business or employ poor people. I do not see that changing anytime soon.

T.D. Did the plantation system play a role in creating poverty?

E.M. According to my understanding, I believe that large factories who wanted to come to Tallahatchie County were waved on because large farmers thought that they would have to increase the salaries to compete with the big industries. Because if you get big industries who are paying more money, then people are going to go to them. And so the county government wouldn't let that happen. Heat Craft was one of the factories that was waved on and it went to Grenada because of that. The farmers fought it. The White Citizens Council fought it.

T.D. What about people who left the plantation and didn't have the education needed to work in the industries?

E.M. There are no jobs in Tallahatchie County. The school system and the corrections system [penitentiary system] are the biggest employers in Tallahatchie County. If you are not a school teacher or a custodian in the school system or working in the penitentiary system, there really are no jobs. I guess the Tallahatchie County hospital is also one of the biggest employers now.

T.D. You are County Supervisor now and blacks have been able to gain some positions like that. Is that enough to change things?

E.M. I'll tell you, we have blacks on the Board of Supervisors but they will not stand up for the black community. They are just going along. That is one reason I ran against Mr. Jerome Little, who I respect a whole lot, but after he got on the board, to me, he was trying to go along. And I understand that when you are in a system and you're trying to get these three votes needed, but I have to get something out of it for my community too. So, I didn't feel that they were fighting for their community. I ran against a young black man that was on the Board of Supervisors, Carey Hayes, Jr., and I beat him. The first question that I or a black person should ask if he's going to run against another black person is what can you do that he is not doing? Or what is he doing that you could do better? Have you ever asked for anything and he didn't do it? Have you ever been to a board meeting? When he got on the board he was manipulated. And they put a lot of money into his campaign. It was hard for me to beat him. I did have some white support. They wanted engineers from Tallahatchie County, but the engineer they hired was from Sunflower County. I've always chose, if possible, people from our own county.

T.D. How were you elected judge?

E.M. It was a tough race. I beat a white female, Kim Newton, by about 40 votes. After that, they never came close to beating me because the judge situation was a situation where I had seen a lot of abuse. I had seen deputy sheriffs who owned a bail bond company setting bond and people had to pay it. Tallahatchie County had this system and we had to go to the federal court to stop that. If you sat in jail you had to pay $10 a day. We challenged that and won in a federal court. They have a motto that if you stay out of the ground, they would keep you out of the jail. So, people were cutting and shooting people and doing all kinds of things because of this system. As judge I was able to set bond for people and change this system. One experience I had was that a young man shot his girlfriend. The girl said he was playing with a gun and accidentally shot her. So, they sent this white dude, who was the young man's boss to me to get him out of jail. The boss man asked, "What would it take for me to get that boy out?" I told him, $10,000. He told me Oh no! I'm not paying that because what we used to do is the judge would let me have him on a $10,000 recognizance bond and then I can charge him. He was just that foolish to tell me that. I said well you need $10,000 cash money to get him out. In the past, what they would do was to get someone out on a recognizance bond and then charge the guy $10,000 and he would never get through paying them. So, he would have to work for them the rest of his life. I said no, it don't work like that. So, the family knew me and had been knowing me all of my life. They came to me and said, "Eddie, why did you tell Mr. Jimmy that it's gonna take $10,000 to get him out. The girl say that it was an accident. He's going to lose his job and everything if he can't get out and work."

So, I asked them, what you all want to do. They said we want to get him out. So, I said go tell them I will let them have him on your own recognizance, but let me tell you something. As long as you all been knowing my family, my brother got children in the family and you all would rather go to the white man than to go to me, who you all elected to take care of your business. I said, he aint got no power with me; you all got power with me. So, go and tell him I said turn your son out and let you have your son. You don't need no money to get him out. The man wanted to make them move when they got the boy out and didn't need his help. He didn't get along with them too good after that. But they got their son out of jail and he didn't lose his job because he was a good tractor driver. His boss wanted to get him out on a $10,000 recognizance bond and then make him work to pay off the debt. And that was what they had been doing. Black folks didn't know anything about a recognizance bond when I was judge. They only knew about cash bonds. If they got a little speeding ticket they would tell him he needed a cash bond. So, I said give him a $200 cash bond because that's what the fine was going to be. And if he is found guilty, then that $200 bond will go toward his fine. If you pay a bail bondsman, that $200 is lost. So that helped our community tremendously. Everybody was helped and I didn't have any problem getting elected anymore because our community knew that I was going to stand up for them.

T.D. How many years did you serve as judge?

E.M. Eleven years. I volunteered to step down because I wanted to run for Supervisor because the Sheriff Department and a lot of them were attacking me and the Supervisors wouldn't pay for my attorney. Jerome Little was one of the Supervisors. He was also one of the Magnificent Seven. Since they wouldn't pay for my attorney, I had to spend money out of my pocket. A situation came up on a judicial performance matter. They said that I needed to apologize to the deputy. I told them that my father taught me not to apologize for something that I didn't do. It was about a case where they were running in black folks houses kicking in doors at two and three o'clock in the morning scaring people to death with guns and flashlights. But they were trying to circumvent my court by going to the east side of the county to get the warrants after going and searching people's houses. I didn't like that so the community circulated a petition and I signed my name on it, which was wrong. But all of the cases that came after that with that deputy, I turned over to the grand jury to settle the case. Well, he felt that I shouldn't have heard his case because I had signed my name on that petition. So, I didn't apologize, so they filed a judicial performance charge against me that went to the Mississippi Supreme Court. The people told me that it would cost $10,000 to get a lawyer. However, I had an attorney friend in Clarksdale, Oscar Shaw, who represented me for $1,800. He let me pay him $900 down and the rest on installment until I paid it out. The Mississippi Supreme Court ruled in my favor.

T.D. What was the charge against you?

E.M. They said it was impropriety in office because I signed the petition and I was a judge. I signed the petition because I didn't like the way they were trying to circumvent the court on the west side of the county where I had jurisdiction as judge by getting a warrant on the east side of the county to search houses on the west side of the county. I understand that judges have to avoid impropriety, and also the appearance of impropriety. So, I retired from judge to run for County Supervisor because Mr. Little and them paid the legal expenses for the sheriff but did not pay mine. So, he didn't vote for me and I was in his district and he and I were supposed to be down with it. So, I resigned from judge and ran against him for County Supervisor. He beat me, but I sent a very important message to him and the rest.

T.D. Tell me what you remember about the Emmett Till case.

E.M. We had one of the Magnificent Seven who was involved. His name was L.D. Willis. He told us everything about what happened to the kid and the trial that he was able to attend because white people knew him and trusted him. He told us that they lynched the little black kid because some white woman said he had whistled at her. That was all I needed to know because Tallahatchie County has had some heinous stuff to happen. A lot of it still has not been taken care of. When I was president of the NAACP, I think we got more missing bodies and missing people than any area in the State of Mississippi. One case I worked on was the Ashley Hankins case in Charleston. We asked for an investigation about the house that was burned down where he was last seen in—a white person's house; they were drug addicts. And there was the Gladys Sauce case where a boy was supposed to kill her, his doctor, Jim Bo Lewis, and his daddy was a doctor, and Tallahatchie County did not pursue the case. I imagine that all of the evidence is now gone. Tallahatchie County is a very difficult place to live in. Emmett Till was some kind of tragedy; the way L.D. told us black people were sitting right up in the courthouse and whites, including Sheriff Strider, were blatantly calling them niggers. We got a chance to beat his nephew in an election real bad;

in a contest of nine people he was the incumbent, but came in about 6th or 7th place. He was one of them who was giving Johnny B. all of the hell. They locked Johnny B. up, raided his café, took all of his beer and stuff and carried it to a Nazi camp and they sat around and drunk it all up.

T.D. How did the descendants of Milam, Bryant, Sheriff Strider and their relatives get along with blacks in the area?

E.M. Most of them had learned pretty much how to treat black folks. Blacks and whites don't socialize in Tallahatchie County very much. There is very little socializing between black and white people here. In fact, there is very little in the State of Mississippi, and there is very little in Tallahatchie County. The ones who do, socialize with them as their employers. They work on white folks' farms and that's about it. Johnny Bryant is the only one that I know that is a descendant of the Bryants that was involved in the Emmett Till case. He is the mayor of the town of Sumner, up there where the courthouse is where the trial was held. He made a statement one day when Johnny B. and myself were up there when they had brought this Beckwith man back to stand trial for the murder of Medgar Evers. He stated that, "They need to bring him (Evers) on down here so we can take care of this," referring to the Emmett Till Murder. After making that statement, before he died, he had a black woman caregiver that was putting diapers on him when he couldn't even go to the bathroom for himself.

T.D. Can you tell me about your involvement in the Civil Rights Movement?

E.M. We made quite a bit of progress when I was president of the NAACP. I was the first male president of the Tallahatchie County NAACP. All of the rest had been women, such as Lucy Boyd, Birda Keglar, just women who were at the front. I never understood that. Maybe they were braver and less of a threat to the white folks. During my tenure as NAACP president, we boycotted our school system. Dr. Morris Kinsey was the State NAACP Education Committee Chairman. Dr. Kennedy came down and we boycotted our school system. What we had was black kids and families were not able to use the school campus. White kids who went to the private schools could go to the campus and play baseball and softball, on the fields. We also found that Tallahatchie County was buying license plates and engines for the buses for private schools and were taking care of private schools better than they were taking care of the public schools. The private schools were all white. The white school was Strider Academy. So you can imagine how that was because they were the descendants of the same Strider that was involved in the Emmett Till case. So, they were taking care of private schools with public school funds. We had a lot of white school board members whose children were in private schools, but we made them get off the board. And we had a lot of teachers who were working in the private schools who could then come back out and work in the public schools a few years and then retire and get retirement. We cut that to a minimum during my tenure as NAACP president. I had some good people with me, Johnny B. Thomas, Gyrone Kenniel, Robert Huddleston, Jerome Little, Richard Gardner, and L.D. Willis. We were members of the Magnificent Seven, an organization that fought for civil rights for black people in the area. Yolanda Harris was the secretary for the organization. We got it to the point that children and parents had more access to the schools to use for public gatherings. You don't have any facilities, so why not let the people use the schools. Staff members would monitor the use of the school facilities. We made quite a few changes and it was through the NAACP that a lot of our lawsuits were filed.

T.D. Could you tell me about your relationship with Mayor Johnny B. Thomas?

E.M. My relationship with Mayor Thomas is that we are good friends. One time I was about to lose my house and Mayor Thomas helped me save my house. He's just that kind of friend. And he still is a good friend to me. When he did his little short stay in jail, I was the best friend that he ever had. When law enforcement was trying to mess with him, I was one of the best friends he ever had because I was basically, down there with him all the time. Mayor Thomas is a hard driver and once he gets his mind set on something, that's what he's going to do. He's going to drive it home. He is an advocate, a strong advocate for black folks. That's the bottom line. I think that is one reason he has some of the hard times that he has because he is not gonna change. He's gonna speak out if he needs to. Some people don't like that but that's the way it is. Johnny don't care if you like it or not. He's gonna do what he's got to do. He stuck with that little old town [Glendora]. If it wasn't for him, I don't know nobody else that wanted to stay there in that little town. He is dedicated to that little town. His town like other towns has struggled, especially since it has come under black control, and his town has been under black control for a long time. So, you know he has been struggling. But Johnny B. singlehandedly brought the Corrections Corporation to Tallahatchie County, the biggest industry we have. All of us were fighting it. We didn't want that type of industry here. We wanted Wackenhut. But Johnny went and met with the guys and got us flown out to Washington D.C. and got the guy, Joe Johnson, to fly down here, who was on the Board of Directors. And when the deal come down, Johnny got his way and we all fell in line with the Corrections Corporation, which is a penitentiary system. They own about a 60 million dollars piece of property and the County get right at $600,000 in property taxes off it. At one time we were getting 1.2 million dollars a year in per diem for inmates that they housed there, but now it has been cut down drastically. But Mayor Thomas fought to bring it here.

A lot of redistricting that we were able to do most times went with what Mayor Thomas wanted instead of what we wanted because he was more experienced in it and he knew how to run it. He was probably the first black person ever to be elected to anything here in Tallahatchie County.

T.D. Are most of the inmates at the penitentiary black?

E.M. No, they have Mexicans and Puerto Ricans and others who are all from out of state. Now, I am sure that nationwide that may be the case. I worked up there at the pen. When I resigned from judge and after I lost the election for County Supervisor, I worked up there for a few months and then worked at the Delta Correctional Facility in Greenwood where I taught carpentry to inmates.

84

T.D. How many people are employed at the Corrections Corporation?

E.M. I think it is roughly 400 and most of them are from the Delta—Leflore County, Coahoma County, Sunflower County, Quitman County, and Tallahatchie County.

T.D. What other industries are located in Tallahatchie that create jobs for people?

E.M. I've been trying to work on some economic development. If you want to hear the truth, it's not that many people interested in doing anything because our board is kind of old fashioned. We got a bunch of farmers on the board and they don't seem to be concerned about industry and stuff like that. You got three farmers and one black guy and they don't seem to worry about bringing in industries. I've been meeting and going to community meetings trying to see what we can do to get some type of industry here. If we can get an industry that employs 20 people that would be a good start. But I don't want to see a big industry come here that employs 300 or 400 people because when it leaves, that's how many jobs will leave. If you can get five industries here and each employs five here and five there, that's the way we see development is needed.

T.D. How many County Commissioners are there in Tallahatchie County?

E.M. Five. Two are black and three are white. But the county as a whole is about 65% black. One white got elected in a majority black district. It's all about the way the [district] lines are drawn. You got the municipality of Charleston which has a black mayor that was finally elected. According to the attorney who does redistricting, if they redistrict in the county, it would knock one of the white guys out because it would make those districts more competitive.

T.D. Is there anything else you would like to tell me?

E.M. Yes. I would like to say that Johnny B. is and always has been a fighter for his community and for that town down there and for

Tallahatchie County. I just want to make sure he gets recognition for that. I don't know nobody that I respect more than him for the way he stands on things. A lot of times I will start an argument with him just to hear what he thinks.

T.D. Thank you very much for the interview.

01/05/2004

Patrice Brown, Shirley Thomas, Actress Ruby Dee, Patricia Brown, and Mona Collie Lee at groundbreaking ceremony for Museum, 2004.

Visitors at the museum from Calvary Missionary
Baptist Church, New York City, 2004.

Antique farming equipment used on plantations in Tallahatchie Parish.

Mayor Thomas and Cory Booker at Brother's Keeper
Conference, Washington, D.C., February, 2015.

Congressman Bennie Thompson and Mayor Thomas
assist in youth development activities in Glendora.

Exhibit in the Emmett Till Museum in Glendora, 2011.

Mayor Thomas at 2nd Inauguration of President
Barack Obama, Washington, D.C., 2012.

Dr. Miriam Clarke and Dr. Mary Crockett of Calvary Baptist Church of New York City visit Emmett Till Museum with Mayor Thomas, 2004.

Youth visit Emmett Till Museum with Tour Guide, Mayor Thomas, 2012.

Exhibit at Emmett Till Museum in Glendora, 2011.

Deputy Walter Hawkins, First African American
Deputy Sheriff of Tallahatchie County.

Attorney General Eric Holder and Mayor Thomas at Brother's
Keeper Conference, Washington, D.C., February, 2015.

Adeline Hill, Mother of Johnny B. Thomas, at
the restaurant she owned in Glendora.

Black Bayou Bridge where Emmett Till's Body was discarded in 1955.

Old Firestone Service Station in Glendora where Clinton
Melton was murdered by Elmer Kimbell in 1956.

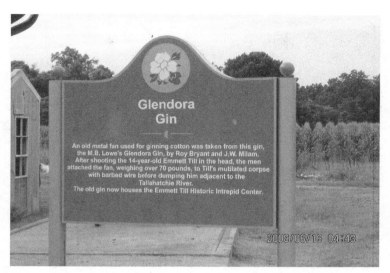

Glendora Gin Historic Marker donated by Actor Morgan Freeman.

The Glendora flood of 1932.

Glendora Methodist Church.

Graduation of Prentiss Williams with father, Johnny Thomas.

Henry Lee Loggins, father of Johnny Thomas and
alleged accomplice in murder of Emmett Till.

Sign at the Emmett Till Historic Intrepid Museum,
designed by Latasha Nicole Suggs, 2005.

Sonny Boy Williamson Bed & Breakfast, and former
House of Marion Lowe, 2nd mayor of Glendora.

Congressman John Lewis of Atlanta and Mayor Thomas
at Mississippi Policy Conference, Tunica, MS, 2011.

Mayor Thomas and Emmett Till's cousin,
Airicka Gordon.

Mayor Thomas and Emmett Till's cousins
at Sumner Courthouse, 2007.

Dorothy Moore, Senator Thad Cochran, Mayor Thomas,
and Devry Anderson at Sumner Courthouse.

Judge Margaret Carey McCrae and Mayor Thomas
at Emmett Till Museum in Glendora, 2011.

Matriarchs of Glendora: Emma Fletcher, Lucille
Syas, and Shirley Thomas (all deceased).

Ida Mae Thomas celebrates her 65th birthday with friend Gracie
Scooter, at Sonny Boy Williamson Bed & Breakfast, 2006.

Mayor Thomas and Trina George, first African
American female Executive Director of USDA.

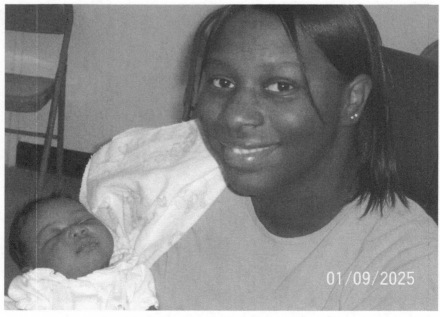

Marsheka Smith and baby, daughter and
granddaughter, of Mayor Thomas.

Tequila Chairse, Pearlie Hodges, Catherine Bridges, Aquarius Simmons, and Yolanda Anderson receive Computer Technology Training Certificates from Mayor Thomas, 2010.

King's Place Juke Joint exhibit at Emmett Till Museum, 2005.

Visitor at the Emmett Till Museum, 2005.

Lurene Suggs and Mary Morgan (principal donors), and tour
guide, Shirley Thomas, at Emmett Till Museum, 2005.

Open Air exhibits of antiques at Emmett Till Museum, 2005.

Mayor Thomas conducts tour of the Emmett Till
Museum with Shirley Thomas and visitor, 2005.

01/03/2004

Visitors at the Emmett Till Museum, 2005.

TO MY NEXT BIG BROTHER

Former U.S. President William "Bill" Clinton and
Mayor Thomas meet in Clarksdale, MS, 2007.

Scene of train derailment that spilled 30,000
gallons of diesel fuel in Glendora in 2005.

Grandson and son (Robert Johnson, Jr.) of famed blues singer
Robert Johnson, with Mayor Thomas in Holly Springs, MS.

CHAPTER 9

THE EMMETT TILL MEMORIAL COMMISSION

THE EMMETT TILL Memorial Commission was formed in 2007 by the County Board of Supervisors, under the leadership of its president, Jerome G. Little. The purpose of the Commission was to seek truth and justice in the Emmett Till murder and trial and promote healing and racial reconciliation in Tallahatchie County. In 2007, Mayor Robert Grayson of Tutwiler and Mrs. Betty Pearson, chair and co-chair of the Emmett Till Memorial Commission, invited the public to the opening ceremony of the Commission. They sent a letter inviting the public to the opening ceremony of the Emmett Till Memorial Commission that would be held on September 24, 2007 on the steps of the courthouse in Sumner, Mississippi where the murder trial was held 52 years earlier on September 19, 1955.

In addition to announcing the opening of the Commission, the purpose of the ceremony was to seek public participation and involvement in racial healing and reconciliation for the injustices that occurred during the Emmett Till murder and trial. The members of the Commission realized more than 50 years ago the justice system at all levels failed to achieve justice in the Emmett Till case and the people in the area had not fully acknowledged the injustices that had been done and the need for reconciliation. The Commissioners wanted to provide an opportunity for the people to express their regrets and pledge to never let this type of injustice happen again. They also wanted to show the world that the shameful murder and trial that happened in their community were a part of the past and they were ready to repair the damaged relationships and move forward. However, the Commission realized that much work needed to be done to accomplish this task.

People from the local communities in Tallahatchie and political representatives from the Delta were invited to the opening ceremony, including U. S. Congressman Bennie Thompson and Senator David Jordan. Congressman Thompson, who supported the cause of the Commission, stated that the Emmett Till murder and trial was an unfortunate chapter in the history of Mississippi, but it "should not be swept under the rug" because it did happen. He also stated that there is need for "preservation of history," as well as "reconciliation." Senator David Jordan also supported the Commission. Jordan was one of the four students from Mississippi Valley State University who attended the murder trial in Sumner. He spoke of the racial tension and segregation and the circus-like atmosphere in the courtroom where the trial was held. He observed the grueling cross-examination of Mr. C.A. Miller, the African American who picked up the body and brought it to Greenwood, by the defense attorney, who tried to discredit his testimony that the disfigured body was that of Emmett Till. Because of the ring on Till's finger with the initials L.T., it was finally concluded that it was Emmett Till's body.

Dr. Marvin Haire, Director of the Delta Research and Cultural Institute at Mississippi Valley State University spoke at the ceremony. He mentioned his work in advising the Emmett Till Memorial Commission with organizational and historical documentation. Dr. Haire was very helpful as a consultant in helping with the development of the Emmett Till Historic Intrepid Center and the Emmett Till Memorial Trail. He provided technical assistance to these projects, including grant writing, research, and oral histories. Much of the research that he conducted on the Emmett Till case was used by the Emmett Till Memorial Commission.

Reverend Wheeler Parker, Emmett Till's cousin, who witnessed the kidnapping of Till, returned to Mississippi from Chicago and made remarks at the opening ceremony of the Commission. Reverend Wheeler was a major force in achieving some measure of racial peace and reconciliation. He stated that he nor Mrs. Mobley-Till was not bitter or held any animosity towards the whites who murdered Till or their descendants because hate destroys the lives of people. Although it was probably very difficult for her, Emmett Till's mother was not bitter and turned a negative into a positive by starting the Emmett Till Foundation. However, he felt strongly that they must keep the Emmett Till Memorial legacy alive so that history will never repeat itself. He was also highly impressed by the courage of the great granddaughter of Sheriff Clarence Strider, who attended the ceremony. Her great grandfather made racist remarks and actions against blacks during the Till murder and trial.

Sussanne Buttrey, the great granddaughter of Sheriff Clarence Strider also attended the ceremony. She was one of the few whites who attended the ceremony. She acknowledged the racist nature of her family and that all of her life, she grew up hearing about the Emmett Till murder and trial, mostly from the side of her family. She stated that despite the fact that the Emmett Till murder and trial hung over her family "like a black cloud," she "always spoke out against racism" and racial segregation and encouraged people to step up and "do something about it to change it."

Jerome G. Little, County Commissioner and a member of the Emmett Till Memorial Commission, made a passionate plea for help from President Barack Obama for preservation of the legacy of Emmett Till, especially the preservation of the historic funeral home at Tutwiler and the historic Bryant's Grocery so that people across the nation could learn about the role of the Emmett Till case in the Civil Rights Movement.

Former Governor William Winters stressed the importance of education about the Emmett Till case and the history of Mississippi. He stated that although we have come a long way, a lot more need to be done in the Delta and that it should be done "by the people who live here." He also emphasized the importance of tourism, "learning from the past," and to "not live in the past." He stated that the past should give us lessons on "how to conduct ourselves in the future."

Echoing William Winter's support for tourism, Page Hunt, Executive Director of the Greenwood Convention and Visitor's Bureau, emphasized the need for preservation of Bryan's Grocery Store and other historic structures related to the Emmett Till case to promote tourism. She stressed the need to learn from history so that the negative part of history will not repeat itself. She stated that the Emmett Till story provided the "perfect" opportunity to talk about the Civil Rights Movement, while respecting the memory of Emmett Till.

The members of the Commission included Mayor Robert Grayson of Tutwiler (Chair), who was raised on the Pearson plantation; Betty Pearson (Co-Chair); Sykes Sturdivant and Martha Ann Sturdivant, who owned one of the largest and wealthiest plantations in the area; Bobby Banks, County Supervisor, who was raised on the Mitchner Plantation, who I ran against three times and lost because he had support from the whites; a former judge, who was not very active in civic matters; and Johnny B. Thomas, who was raised on the Flautts plantation. A few individuals were added to the Commission at different times. Susanna Buttrey and several other whites were added in an attempt to achieve racial balance on the Commission.

The members of the Commission held periodic meetings to determine the course of action to achieve its goals. Everybody was afraid of me because I was outspoken and a member of the NAACP. They called me radical. In my view, we needed some liberal-minded people on the Commission, and grass roots people, not five million dollar plantation owners like Ricky Betts and Sykes Sturdivant, who tried to use their economic and political influence to sway votes and decisions. These were people who opposed me in the election for County Supervisor because they thought my views were too radical. One of the members told me "Boy, they are gonna kill you because you talk too much." We also needed representatives from all of the churches. Ironically, the Commission was formed 40 years too late, after the murder of Emmett Till and the trial of his killers. However, the Commission attempted to bring the black and white descendants of the Emmett Till murder together to find peace, forgiveness, and closure.

I was a member of the Commission with Susanna Buttrey, the great-grand-daughter of Sheriff Clarence Strider, who was the sheriff of Tallahatchie County when Emmett Till was murdered and during the time of the murder trial. I think she joined the Commission because she wanted something different said about her great-grandfather. I know that I wanted something different said about my father, other than him being an accomplice in the murder of Emmett Till, to explain if he had been forced by his boss, J. W. Milam, to participate in the murder of Emmett Till, and why he secretly left town before the murder trial of Bryant and Milam. The members of the Commission believed that my father was an accomplice to the murder of Till, but I believed that he was forced by Milam to participate in the murder. However, the whole story was distorted, twisted, changed, or covered up. Some people still have a KKK mentality and do not want to deal with the past realities and issues surrounding the Till murder and how it impacted the black and white people of the communities in Tallahatchie County. Of course, this mentality still exists among some people who do not want to tell the truth about what they know about the Emmett Till murder. They want to sweep their dirty past under the rug, and then pretend everything is alright. However, I felt that we had to acknowledge and deal with this dirty past if we were going to be able to heal and move on. It is amazing that more than sixty years after the Till murder, we are still being haunted by this tragedy.

Shortly after the whites joined the Commission, one of them proposed a 50-50 racial makeup, and this was approved by the members. I had an uneasy feeling about the whites coming in and trying to dictate the rules. I was also upset because I thought the Commission was not aggressive enough, and there was not enough participation by the members. The few whites on the Commission wanted to control everything. It was always a heated debate between me and the few white members, but the other African American members made little expression of what they wanted to see, in terms of the direction that the Commission should take. I was the most outspoken African American on the Commission, which turned off both blacks and whites. They thought that my suggestions were too radical and controversial.

I was elected treasurer of the Commission, but some of the members opposed my election, stating that I could not serve as treasurer because I had been to prison on a federal misdemeanor. But how can I be bonded as Mayor of Glendora and not be bonded as treasurer on the Commission? I was furious and told them, "Dam the Commission! This is worse than Jim Crowism, right here today in Tallahatchie County, Mississippi." Everyone knew that I served four months in federal prison for operating slot machines. But slot machines were operating all over Tunica and Tallahatchie Counties, and the sheriff was running a country club that had lots of slot machines. I had slot machines in my club in Glendora, but I was busted because of racism. I was considered a black radical who got out of his place and had to be punished. During the days of slavery, blacks were beaten or lynched; now, they are sentenced to prison time where they work for the state. There were about 50 or 60 people operating slot machines in Tallahatchie County, but they only sent me to prison. They did not want black people to share in the wealth. They wanted to keep us down. They made a scapegoat out of me. We are still suffering for the sins of our fathers.

I wanted the Commission to explore how the children of those involved in the Emmett Till case survived, including the children of my father, who they say was involved in the Emmett Till murder right from the beginning. I wanted the Commission to find out about people in both families who were affected by the murder of Emmett Till. Some of the black families were sinful too in some of the things they did, but I feel that our conditions were created by Jim Crowism, while the white families benefitted from Jim Crowism, intentionally or unintentionally. I wanted to bring the sins of our fathers to light.

I was interested in finding out how the kids of Roy Bryant and J.W. Milam survived after the sins of their fathers. Both sides were affected by the Jim Crow customs, although in different ways. This is something that I wanted to bring forward. We all lived in the same area. Their children were the same ages as me and my siblings. At times we rolled tires together and played in the dirt together, because we lived just out the back door from each other. My family lived in a little two-room shotgun house right out the back door from the Milam family. The kids of Bryant and Milam lived in the area at the time of the murder and trial and were affected by all that happened. My intent for being on the Commission was to help bring together the children of Milam, Bryant, Sheriff Strider, and the black families to see if we could create some type of racial reconciliation and healing.

I suggested that we bring in Oprah Winfrey to mediate the breaking of bread together to bring about racial healing and racial reconciliation for all of the people who were suffering from the sins of our fathers. However, some of the members of the Commission demeaned my suggestions and my aggressive language. I was viewed as hostile and made a villain because I spoke out about issues concerning the past atrocities committed against blacks. I spoke out because I felt that in order for racial healing to take place we needed to face the truth about the past, the truth about the role that our ancestors played in the murder of Emmett Till, and the injustices done in the trial of Roy Bryant and J.W. Milam for the murder of Till by the all-white jury. How can we move forward to the future without confessing the past?

CHAPTER 10
THE COMMUNITY REVITALIZATION MOVEMENT

THE SAYING THAT "there is no place like home" could characterize the beliefs of most of the families who live in Glendora, who have longtime family roots in the town. It does not matter if Glendora has been defined as a poor village with a high percentage of the residents living below the poverty line. It does not matter that the town has been described by outsiders as "barely more than a group of homes, with some ramshackled store fronts, strung along a few narrow streets with no yellow lines, no curbs, no sidewalks, and deteriorating buildings." And it does not matter that the rate of poverty is among the highest in the State and nation, and that unemployment is about 40%. These conditions may lead some to ask, "Can any good come out of Glendora?" Or as one state official asked, "Can Glendora control its own destiny?" With all of these challenges, I was optimistic that Glendora could turn its situation around, "if we can bring more development to the community. I also believe that our youth can help make a difference."

For years, the town of Glendora has searched for a viable project that could significantly improve the economic development of the town and the quality of life of the residents. A few years ago, the town tried raising sweet potatoes, but had limited success. Although there was an abundance of available land for crop production, the major challenge was finding adequate labor and capital to sustain a farming enterprise. There simply was not enough interest in farming to support a viable crop production operation. Thus, there was little hope that conventional agriculture was the answer to community development in Glendora.

Glendora, in collaboration with Youth Opportunity Unlimited, received a federal grant from the Youth Bill that provided for the creation of the Youth Opportunities Unlimited project. In this program, selected youth were chosen to travel to various metropolitan cities around the country to tour and attend professional basketball, football, and baseball games. The town also started a Cottage Industries for Youth program and obtained a Community Connect grant for training local residents how to operate a computer and introducing wireless internet services into every home in the community. These were just a few of the community development projects that assisted residents in employment and vocational training. The limitation of these programs was that they could not be sustained because of the lack of local funds to maintain them. When the funds ran out, so did the programs. Thus, town officials of Glendora continued to search for a project that could bring sustainable economic development to the town. We were determined to find a lucrative enterprise to support economic development and community revitalization, and vowed that the town would never return to the "mountain of despair" that characterized much of its past. But the real question was what type of development project could achieve this goal?

Fortunately, in 2004, the town of Glendora applied for and received a sizeable grant of $375,000 from the United States Department of Agriculture to develop a Community Technology Center that included a broadband communication system. Could this be the answer that the town had been waiting on for their deliverance? Would it bring sustainable development to the town? Town officials were aware of the rapidly expanding movement toward computer technology. The expansion of wireless internet systems made communication technology more accessible to small rural communities, and Glendora wanted to be a part of it in a way that could be beneficial to the town and its residents. A development committee, with technical assistance from representatives from the AbsoCom Corporation, a minority-owned technology services vendor in Jackson, Mississippi, explored the possibility of developing a Community Technology Center (CTC) for the operation of a broadband network. AbsoCom conducted a community survey to determine the feasibility of developing a broadband communication system that would be housed in a Community Technology Center. The results of the survey provided information that was useful in designing a project that could yield positive benefits to the community. The planning for the network was done by members of a Steering Committee appointed by the mayor. The Steering Committee agreed that Mayor Johnny Thomas would make all committee appointments and approve all positions of the Community Technology Center.

The Community Technology Center was housed in the old abandoned cotton gin that had been renovated for use as a multi-purpose community center that would also house the Emmett Till and Sonny Boy Williamson II cultural tourism project. The Center included adult classes, after school tutorial programs, special projects, e-mails, online research, and a Wi-Fi network component that used radio towers to cover several square miles with high speed wireless coverage. The Center and the computer network system were owned by the community and had the potential of providing internet services to other municipalities in the area. Ms. Danielle Miller, a local resident was appointed as the Community Support Technician, Manager, and Operator of the Center, with guidance from the Steering Committee, which was comprised of residents of the community, including Tracy Bridges, Tracy Rosebud, and Danielle Miller (Chair).

Everyone was excited when the Community Technology Center opened with a full house of participants from the community. The first eight graduates completed the computer training in 2007. Now, the challenge was to keep the momentum going and increase the sustainability of the Center by maintaining participation of residents, maintaining services, and gradually expanding the network into other communities in the area. If successful, the Community Technology Center in Glendora could serve as a model for wireless broadband networks in small rural communities in the Mississippi Delta. The Community Technology Center could also provide internet services that could attract new businesses and services to the town, such as fax and copy services, internet access, job training, social work services, and tourism. In regard to the latter, the Community Technology Center could potentially provide an internet grid to support other cultural heritage sites in the vicinity, such as the Mule Train Museum in Marks, Fannie Lou Hamer Memorial Park and Museum in Ruleville, and the Emmett Till Museum and the "Sonny Boy" Williamson Blues Heritage site in Glendora. The plan was to integrate these tourist sites into a website as an e-commerce page for tourism planning and scheduling that would be managed by technicians of the Community Technology Center in Glendora.

There was great hope that the wireless communication system, combined with a cultural tourism program, would be the "shot in the arm" that Glendora needed to propel the town into a higher level of economic development and contribute to community revitalization. We were optimistic about the prospects of the center and believed that the CTC project could help create jobs that could break the cycle of out-migration of youth and working age residents, and also attract new residents to the town.

Unfortunately for Glendora, the broadband internet project was discontinued after three years of operations (2011-2014). The project failed due to lack of training for the community as outlined in the grant, and failure of the consultant (AbsoCom) to carry out its part of the project that caused the entire project to fail. In addition, the partnership with AbsoCom did not work out as planned because AbsoCom wanted to convert the project into a corporate operation that would be owned by corporate partners, who would have full control of the project. However, I refused to accept corporate ownership of the project because the original plan called for community ownership. Consequently, AbsoCom severed its ties to the project and discontinued the training and construction of the call center, the internet system, the communication system, and other components necessary to operate the project. When the project ended, only five people had received training. Two of these persons decided to stay in Glendora; one moved to Houston; one moved to Atlanta; and one moved to Tutwiler, Mississippi.

CHAPTER 11

CULTURAL HERITAGE TOURISM

A FTER I BECAME Mayor of Glendora in 1982, I began searching for ways to uplift my people and community. There were a lot of poor people living in Glendora; and the situation was made worst by the desertion of the town by white businesses and public officials who feared repercussions from racial desegregation of the public schools and the black voter registration movement. I inherited a town that had been stripped of most of its major economic resources. When the white folks left, they took all of their wealth with them, including their businesses, banks, capital, and other economic resources. They sold their homes to blacks or anyone who had the money to buy them. Glendora largely became a ghost town with an overwhelming majority black population and a high percentage of poor people. Although blacks gained some form of school desegregation and freedom to vote, they lost jobs and economic resources because most of the businesses and financial institutions owned by whites were closed after the white flight from the town.

By 1982, when I became mayor, the population of Glendora had changed from 54% to 99.9% black. The only white family in Glendora lived on their plantation just outside the village, and had little interest or connection to the town. The families that lived in

Glendora were descendants of the families who lived and worked on the large plantations in the area, including Frederick, Sturdivant, Haynes, Equen, Buford, Flautts, Mills, and Swan Lake. Most of the families on these plantations worked as sharecroppers, tenant farmers, or agricultural laborers. My parents were sharecroppers on the Flautts plantation. We were poor with little education because plantation work demanded that we work in the fields to make a living. During cotton cultivation and cotton harvesting times, there was no school because all of the black youth old enough to work had to help pick the cotton or do other chores on the plantation. Our livelihood depended on our labor and making a good cotton crop. The demise of sharecropping and the mechanization of plantation agriculture left in its wake a high percentage of displaced laborers, many of whom were left impoverished with little education or economic resources. Many former sharecroppers moved to urban areas in the North and some settled in Glendora and other small town in the Delta. By the time sharecropping ended in the 1960s, a vicious intergenerational cycle of poverty had been ingrained in the area. Such was the case among many of the black families of Glendora and Tallahatchie County.

Shortly after I became Mayor of Glendora, I and the town officials formed a non-profit 501(c)3 corporation named the Glendora Economic and Community Development Corporation (GECDC) to help improve the economic conditions of the residents. Most of the property of the town, including the cotton gin and the building next to it, the park, and the house where the former mayor lived were placed under the ownership of the corporation. The GECDC was established after I discovered that the previous mayor had reduced the tax millage of the town to about $200,000 per year, which was grossly inadequate to meet the needs of the town, and the state government had passed a law that limited the growth of the millage by no more than 10% annually. This action limited the revenue for the town and put the town on the road to extinction. That's when we developed the GECDC to help keep Glendora alive and functioning. Because of the property owned by the corporation, we were able to use it as in-kind to leverage fundraising to help in the development of the community. However, over the years, the town struggled to find a major project for community economic development in Glendora.

Contributing to the impoverished condition of the town was the failure of the Illinois Central Railroad Company to pay taxes to the town for use of town land for the railway. The town needed some type of niche that could bring sustainable economic growth to the town that could help the very poor.

For more than twenty years, the town had pursued small projects with only limited success, such as sweet potato production and a low income housing project. However, in 2005, I discovered a project that I thought had the potential to stimulate economic development in Glendora, during my attendance at the National Council of Black Mayors Conference in Denver, Colorado. There was considerable discussion about the need for economic revitalization of the towns where blacks served as mayors. One of the projects proposed by the group was to provide support for the development of cultural tourism as a means of economic development in these towns. After the conference, I returned to Glendora with the idea that we could use our historic cultural sites and events to develop a cultural tourism project. I discussed the idea of cultural tourism with my family and my staff in the mayor's office.

Somehow the spirit kept coming to me about the Emmett Till case. Every now and then something would crop up about the case, including some of the mysteries that still existed and the families in the area who remembered many of the details about the Till murder, the trial of the offenders, and the impact they had on the local and national civil rights movements. I had a vision to establish a museum centered around the Emmett Till story that could be used for the education and motivation of visitors about the tragic lynching of Emmett Till that could serve as a memorial, place of healing, and a center for education on the events that sparked the Civil Rights Movement. There were ancestors, relics, stories, memories, and mysteries surrounding the Emmett Till murder and trial that still abounded in the area that could be used to achieve this goal.

Although the Emmett Till murder and trial would be the main attraction for tourists, we also wanted the museum to promote education about the life, culture, and history of the people who lived in the area, including plantation life, sharecropping, the effects of Jim Crow customs, and plantation churches that make up the colorful tapestry of the culture of Glendora and the surrounding area. I also thought that the museum could be used for preservation and education of the legendary blues singer and native son, Aleck "Rice" Miller, known as Sonny Boy Williamson II, king of the blues harmonica, and the King's Place Juke Joint, known as the "Las Vegas" of Tallahatchie County. The museum could also be used as a community center for adult education and for training youth in computer education, using a broadband computer network.

Right away, we knew that the main challenge would be to sell the idea to the people and then find the revenue to build the museum. After listening to my proposal, the residents of Glendora were very receptive to the idea of building the museum; however, everyone wanted to know where would a small, rural, poor town get the money to build the museum, and if the museum was built, would it attract tourists in sufficient numbers to generate revenue for the development of the town? The town of Glendora did not have the funds to develop the museum to promote cultural tourism and economic development. The National Council of Black Mayors promised to provide funds for the development of the project, but for some reason the funds were never granted. We thought about trying to secure funds from the Tallahatchie County Commission, but since the 1960s, the town of Glendora had been largely abandoned by the Commission and the State of Mississippi, after the whites deserted the town and took mostly all of the economic resources with them. However, we were successful in gaining technical assistance on cultural heritage tourism from Dr. Marvin Haire, director of the Delta Research & Cultural Institute at Mississippi Valley State University.

Although whites had moved out of Glendora, they still controlled the allocation of revenue to the municipalities in Tallahatchie County. And since the white power structure in Tallahatchie County viewed me as a radical and trouble maker, due to my outspoken position to promote black voter registration, civil rights, and independence, the economic squeeze was put on the town of Glendora by the Tallahatchie County Commission, who reduced the allocation of funds to Glendora that could support development projects. Although I was Mayor of Glendora, the County Commission controlled the amount of funds allocated to the different municipalities in the county. Like many of the small towns and communities in the

Mississippi Delta, Glendora is an economically poor town with a black mayor and inadequate economic resources for development of the town. Although we didn't have many economic resources, at least we were in a position to control our own destiny. This was the reason that we decided to venture into cultural heritage tourism. An extensive search was undertaken to locate funds for the development of a cultural heritage project centered around the Emmett Till murder and trial, the music history of legendary blues harmonica singer Sonny Boy Williamson II, sharecropping, and the rich history and culture of the people of Glendora and Tallahatchie County.

The Mississippi Development Authority (MDA) continued to assist the town of Glendora to find a feasible and viable project that could bring sustainable economic development to Glendora. Professional experts from the Asset Development Team of the Mississippi Development Authority conducted a SWOT assessment to determine the prospects for economic development in Glendora. The approach made by the MDA embraced the following philosophy and rationale:

> Traditional community development tends to look at communities as having needs or deficiencies. With this approach, people focus on their deficits, not capabilities. Successful communities don't concentrate on deficiencies or look for outsiders and professionals to fulfill their needs. Successful communities use the talents of people, their web associations, the strengths of institutions, and their available land, property, and economic power to create new opportunities for themselves. In short, they build on their own assets (Asset Development Team, Mississippi Development Authority, SWOT Analysis, 2009).

With the many obstacles and challenges confronting the town of Glendora, the major question was, "What assets were available for an economic development project?" After conducting the needs assessment survey and embracing the above philosophy and strategy, the Asset Development Team of the Mississippi Development Authority recommended that the town of Glendora should use one of its greatest assets, cultural heritage tourism, as a strategy for economic development, as shown in the following assessment:

> Tourism is the strongest asset for economic development in Glendora. The combination of the blues trail, based on Sonny Boy Williamson, and the Civil Rights history of the Emmett Till murder trial, could bring tourists to Tallahatchie County and Glendora, if the proper tourist exhibit is planned, designed, and developed. Another asset is the computer learning center. We would encourage development of its original vision with the professional help of AbsoCom. The Emmett Till Park has the potential of serving the community recreational needs as well as playing a part in future events. (Asset Development Team, Mississippi Development Authority, *SWOT Analysis*, 2009).

Critical comments included in the assessment were as follows:

> Glendora's assets are not being used to full potential. For full development, Glendora needs to become a tourist friendly town with professional assistance, and quality displays. The town needs to be transformed into an attractive, clean, friendly, and safe town if you have any hope of becoming a real tourist town. The current conditions of the outward appearance suggest a people with no hope, no pride of community, and no willingness to make it better (Asset Development Team, Mississippi Development Authority, *SWOT Analysis*, 2009).

The concept of cultural tourism was not new to Glendora. In August 1998, the Sonny Boy Williamson Library and Community Center was dedicated and opened. A total of 17 relatives of Sonny Boy participated in the dedication, including his nephew, two of his nieces, and 14 children. The attendees listened to a brief story of the life of Sonny Boy and some of his famous songs. A sign had been erected earlier with the words that proudly stated, "This Little Village is the home of Sonny Boy Williamson." In addition to the Library, an annual Sonny Boy Williams Blues Festival was held in Glendora. At a strategic planning meeting in October 2005, the planning committee recommended reviving the legacy of Sonny Boy Williamson to make it a major part of Glendora's cultural tourism project as a means of economic development and community revitalization.

The main attraction for the proposed cultural heritage tourism project would be the Emmett Till Historic Intrepid Center, which would include the Emmett Till Museum, a Sonny Boy Williamson blues exhibit, and a technology center. Other components of the cultural heritage tourism project were the Emmett Till National Park and Nature Trail, a new Sonny Boy Williamson Memorial Blues and Cyber Café, and the Glendora Organic Gardens and Greenhouse. Town officials sought to expand the town limits by annexation of land from Tallahatchie County to permit direct access to the Emmett Till Memorial Highway. It was hoped that this would help increase commerce and tourism for Glendora. Other development projects that were planned included revitalization of the commercial district, including opening new retail stores, restaurants, and a new regional farmer's market.

In addition to considering its assets, the town of Glendora also had to address how to eliminate or minimize its liabilities. Accordingly, one of the major liabilities that Glendora had to deal with was the trains that ran through the middle of the town. During an earlier time, hobos could "hop a train" for a free ride out of town to their destination. But now, modern trains run too fast to jump on for a ride and there are strict laws and security surveillance to prevent hoboing a ride on a freight train. Whether by hoboing or paying customers, many people caught the train, passenger and freight, out of the Delta to escape the "blues" of plantation life to seek their fortune elsewhere. In 1970, the Amtrak train depot in Glendora closed and the train no longer stopped in the town, which further isolated the town because no passengers could stop there. People stopped coming to Glendora to catch the train, and no materials or goods were delivered there, which dried up a major source of revenue and business. As the blues singer put it, "My baby is gone and she ain't coming back no more." Or "Every time I hear that lonesome whistle blow, I want to leave this place and never come back no more."

The railway is now operated by the Canadian National Railroad Company and trains make up to 25 trips per day through the middle of the town. The ear-splitting sound of the train's horn and the tremors and rumbles that shake the houses and businesses on a daily basis are a nuisance to the town and bring distress to residents. Because the train runs through the center of the town and only a few yards from homes and businesses, the people live daily with fear of a catastrophic accident that threaten life and health. A few years ago a major train derailment caused extensive damage to the north end of the town which required a major clean up. Moreover, the train tracks and the trains that run on them discourage people from building homes in the town and lower the value of the property in areas near the tracks. There has been talk about reopening the depot, but from all indication, it is not feasible or profitable to do so. The current reality is that Glendora is not a destination for most people to come.

I wish that the tracks could be re-routed out of the community, but I know that is not likely to happen. We have to find a way to live with it or maybe move to another location or restructure the community, which may not be feasible. It is not likely that the trains will leave Glendora. People do not want to build their home near the railroad tracks, and those who already live there have to tolerate the noise or move. For the most part, residents, home owners, and businesses are resigned to the reality of the disruption of their lives by the constant rumbling of the train. What was once a blessing has now become a nuisance or curse.

CHAPTER 12

BUILDING THE EMMETT TILL HISTORIC INTREPID CENTER

I HAVE BEEN ASKED, why build the Emmett Till Historic Intrepid Center and Museum in the town of Glendora, in the Mississippi Delta, rather than in a large city like Memphis, Chicago, or even Jackson, Mississippi? Perhaps the thinking was that by being located in the city the museum would receive more resources and support and would be accessible to more people. However, I felt that the Museum should be located right here in Glendora where Emmett Till was murdered, so that visitors can learn and understand the culture, environment, and conditions of the people and places where the tragedy occurred. The people who murdered Emmett Till were from Glendora and the surrounding area. The place where Till's body was dumped by his killers is located right here near Glendora. The Black Bayou and the Tallahatchie River are natural historic sites where the tragedy took place. Descendants of the families and friends who knew Till still live in this area.

Glendora, in Tallahatchie County, is the land where I was born and where my parents and relatives lived and worked as sharecroppers on the Flautts plantation. And this is the place where young people grow up with few opportunities to make a decent living and raise a family. Back in history, violence and oppression of blacks by whites was a way of life. So people who come to Glendora can learn about the history and culture of the people who live in this area. So, why not locate the museum in Glendora? However, in order to understand the conditions that currently exist in Glendora and Tallahatchie County, one must first gain an understanding of the historical conditions from which the current conditions evolved, including the Native Americans, the coming of European conquerors, traders, and settlers, plantation slavery, post-slavery poverty, sharecropping and subservience agriculture, the struggle to gain civil rights, and life in the post-civil rights era.

Sadly, Tallahatchie County is where two evil white men conceived and executed the murder of a 14-year-old black child named Emmett Till. Till's spirit still lives here, The Tallahatchie River and the Black Bayou still carry the mysteries of the murder, and the land is still stained with the blood of a black boy who was killed by two white men. People still remember the Till case and still talk about the mysteries surrounding the murder and the trial.

This is also the land where a black man named Johnny B. Thomas lives, who was one year and 18 months old when Till was murdered and whose father was an alleged accomplice to the murder of Till. This is the place where area plantations were part of the plantocracy that oppressed the freedom of blacks for centuries and where many blacks have been murdered by white vigilantes. Also, this is the same place where people attended local churches and prayed to God to overcome the oppressive conditions under which they lived and where young people need to come to learn about the history of their ancestors, because if they do not know their history, they are destined to repeat it. Those who visit this area will not only learn about the Emmett Till murder, but also about the way of life of the people and the social, economic, political, and cultural conditions that created the tragedy. This is why I thought that the Emmett Till Museum should be built here in Glendora and why people should come here and learn about it.

All of these things contributed to the current state of life in Glendora, and the conditions that made it possible to establish a museum centered around the Emmett Till tragedy and the culture of poverty that was created and perpetuated by plantation slavery, subsistence agriculture, sharecropping, oppressive laws, and Jim Crow customs. I have always said that if you are given lemons, use them to make lemonade. Can the culture of tragedy and poverty be marketable in the tourism industry? Specifically, would tourists come to Glendora to see a museum build around the murder of Emmett Till and abject poverty created by slavery, sharecropping, and subsistence agriculture and other historical conditions? Despite the odds, I was convinced that with the right approach, planning, development, and marketing, the town of Glendora could make this happen, at least we were going to try.

Now, I was the Mayor of Glendora, the town was controlled by blacks, and we decided that we were going to do something with the property to help in the development of the town. After conducing some research, we found that there were still many untold stories about the Till murder. We discovered that some of the events connected with the murder of Emmett Till occurred right here in Glendora, including the cotton gin where the gin fan was retrieved that was used in the murder and the Black Bayou Bridge from which Till's body was thrown. Glendora was also the home of J.W. Milam, one of the principals in the murder of Emmett Till, and my father, Henry Loggins, was one of his "right hand" men, who was implicated as a forced accomplice in the Till murder. Many of the historic sites and events that surrounded the Till murder are located in Glendora that could be included in a museum to promote education and at the same time promote cultural tourism that could provide a source of revenue for the development of the town of Glendora.

In 2004, we began the planning to build an open air museum in the old cotton gin in Glendora. I sought help from a number of people. Dr. Marvin Haire, of the Delta Research and Cultural Institute at Mississippi Valley State University, gave expertise and technical assistance in the planning and development of the museum and was a member of the Advisory Council. I also received help and support from Congressman Bennie Thompson in locating start-up funds for building the museum. Congressman Thompson was an influential public official and a native of the Mississippi Delta, who knew how to get things done and was willing to help. We discussed how we could make cultural tourism work with a museum that focused on the murder of Emmett Till and the community of Glendora.

The Emmett Till Historic Intrepid Center and Museum
is located in this renovated cotton gin in Glendora.

In 2005, we started an open-air museum in the old converted cotton gin that included exhibits from gifts of items donated by local residents. Mrs. Gloria Dean Jackson donated a plantation bell. A small group comprised of family members, friends, and residents helped to design the museum. My daughter, Latasha Suggs, and I drafted the budget, and Scotty Simmons, Tracy Bridges, and Tracy Rosebud helped develop the exhibits. Mrs. Temita Davis, a consultant from Atlanta, Georgia, was very instrumental in creating exhibits for the opened-air museum. The Black Bayou Consulting Firm of Glendora also helped in the development of the exhibits for the museum. Dr. Marvin Haire of Mississippi Valley State University helped in planning and developing the museum, and professionals from Prairie View A&M University came to help us establish our first time-line of the Civil Rights Movement. The museum was developed inside the same cotton gin that was operated by J.W. Milam, who helped murder Emmett Till during an earlier time. We were left out of the budget by the Republican controlled Congress, but we managed to get some seed money to help with the start-up.

I was the Mayor at the time and Tracy Bridges and Scotty Simmons, who were employed by my office, assisted in the work without compensation. The town had developed a non-profit 501(c)3 agency, Glendora Economic and Community Development Corporation (GECDC), that owned much of the property of the town including the cotton gin and building next to it, the park, and the house where the former mayor lived. The museum was designed to include a civil rights focus because the Emmett Till murder and trial energized the Civil Rights Movement and the quest for equality and justice for African Americans.

The museum was completed late in 2005 and was dedicated on September 20, 2006. An article printed by the Associated Press, carried by the International Herald Tribune, reported that "Mississippi town opens museum honoring Emmett Till, case energized civil rights movement (Associated Press, September 20, 2006). The event was held at a converted cotton gin that included exhibits of family photos, audio-visual archives, oral histories, and a replica of the cotton gin fan that was used to weigh down Till's body when it was dumped into the Black Bayou. Photographs of Emmett Till's mutilated body were also displayed that stunned the nation that a 14-year-old boy could be brutally beaten and murdered for whistling at a white woman.

Till's cousin, Priscilla Sterling, who was present at the event, stated that she wanted the country "to see this moment as a historic event of how far we have come in the civil rights movement and to open people's eyes to the many other injustices that have happened in other places besides the Delta (Associated Press, September 20, 2006). The museum also included space dedicated to legendary blues singer and harmonica player Sonny Boy Williamson II. Over a period of five years, the movement to renovate and expand the museum continued as more information, artifacts, and other item with historic value were donated by people from the surrounding area.

In 2009, we were fortunate to receive a grant in the amount of $400,000 from the Institute of Museums and Library Services of Washington, D.C. for the purpose of building the Emmett Till Historic Intrepid Center that would convert the opened air exhibits into a state-of-the-art museum. We had submitted a budget for more than a million dollars, but it was reduced to $400,000. Congressman Bennie Thompson and Senator Thad Cochran supported the efforts to obtain funding for the construction of the Emmett Till Center. Although the Emmett Till murder and case would be the main attraction for tourists, we also wanted the museum to promote education about the life, culture, and history of the people who live in the area, including plantation life, sharecropping life and culture, poverty amidst affluence, plantation mansions, sharecropper shacks, slave cabins, the effects of Jim Crow, country churches, and natural lakes, bayous, and swamps, all that made up the colorful tapestry of the rural landscape around Glendora.

Although building a museum would be a great challenge, I was willing to venture into this project. Initially, I discussed the idea with my daughter, Latasha Suggs, and she helped me come up with a plan and a name. After pondering the idea for several weeks, she came up with the name Emmett Till Historic Intrepid Center. I had thought about using the term "Interpretive Center" in the title, but Latasha conducted some research on the Emmett Till murder that convinced me that we should use the term "Intrepid Center" to reflect the fact that Emmett Till was fearless in facing death at the hands of his kidnappers. She found that although Emmett was severely beaten, threatened, and tortured by his captors, he never was afraid of his killers, Milam and Bryant. He never surrendered his dignity to his killers despite the beatings, pain, and torture that were inflicted upon him. He lost his life but he never surrendered his will to his killers. The lesson to be gained from Till's heroic action was never be afraid to stand up for freedom and justice, even when your life is in jeopardy. Intrepid also expresses a theme of strength under pressure, under fire, and never surrender to injustices, violence, brutality, or even murder. Dr. Martin Luther King, Jr. taught us the same lesson through his bravery in exposing himself to death by his enemies without fear that he would be murdered. So, my daughter convinced me that the term "Intrepid" should be a part of the name of the museum.

The Dream Becomes Reality

An article in the Mississippi Link news blog read, "Emmett Till's Center re-opens: 'the healing begins.' On September 24, 2011, fifty-six years after a 14-year-old African American, Emmett Till, was murdered by two white men, J.W. Milam and Roy Bryant, for whistling at Bryant's wife, a store clerk, the town of Glendora opened the Intrepid Center. The opening of the center drew people from Mississippi and other states, including Alabama, Arkansas, Florida, Georgia, New Jersey, and North Carolina. The celebration began with a prayer by Dr. G.A. Johnson, followed by a solo by local attorney Renetha Frieson, reflections by The Honorable Judge Margaret Carey-McCray, a resolution from the Glendora Board of Aldermen read by LaCristal Powel, the Glendora Praise team, and letters from U.S. Congressmen John Lewis and Bennie Thompson, and the Mamie Till Mobley Foundation in Chicago, Illinois.

In his opening remarks, Johnny B. Thomas, Mayor of Glendora stated, "Today on behalf of the citizens of Glendora, we want to welcome you to help us initiate the healing. We think it is rightful that the healing should start here because 56 years ago, [the] premeditation started here, and we feel that it is Glendora's place in history to begin the healing – 56 years late. Senator David Jordan (D-Greenwood), who addressed the crowd, applauded Glendora's efforts toward healing, stated, "Healing does not take place unless all of the infection is moved out of the sore." He stated that his house had been shot into in 2011 in Jackson, Mississippi, and a man was run over because he was black. "These things did not happen in 1955; they happened in 2011." Jordan stated further that "The Emmett Till trial was as hideous as the murder; it was the worst in the history of this country, and it is up to us to see that justice is done. It hasn't been done." Temita S. Davis, the Development Specialist, who was secured to spearhead the project, served as the program guide for the grand re-opening. Davis was the manager of an Atlanta-based company called Black Bayou Cultural Heritage Management Services which helped communities like Glendora to preserve their heritage through community development. The mayor and the development team were dressed in black and white to symbolize blacks and whites coming together, and the orange ribbon, which they adorned symbolized the healing process.

The mission of the museum was prominently displayed: "To provide a penetrable, thought-provoking and educational experience; to preserve and promote the historical and cultural heritage of the Town of Glendora, Tallahatchie County and the State of Mississippi in the continued struggle for civil and human rights." A historic marker where Milam's house once stood was erected near the center. It was ironic that the center was built in an old cotton gin in close proximity to the house where Milam lived, worked, and committed the murder of Emmett Till.

CHAPTER 13

GRAND TOUR OF THE THE EMMETT TILL MUSEUM

SINCE THE DOORS of the museum opened, many tours have been conducted for people from around the country and the world. Come take a tour of the Emmett Till Historic Intrepid Center with the docent, Johnny B. Thomas, Executive Director of the Center and Mayor of Glendora.

Welcome to Glendora!

Welcome to Glendora, Mississippi and the Emmett Till Historical Intrepid Center. I am Johnny B. Thomas, the Mayor of Glendora, Executive Director, and your tour guide. *The mission of the museum is to provide valuable education on the history and culture of the town of Glendora and to memorialize the historical significance of the town of Glendora as the birthplace of the civil rights movement in Tallahatchie County, the State of Mississippi, and the nation, to ensure that the civil, human, cultural, and musical heritage not be forgotten, and to promote cultural heritage tourism within the State of Mississippi.*

A lot of people wonder why the word "Intrepid" is included in the name of this center, rather than the word "Interpretive." After doing some research, my daughter came up with the name "Intrepid Center" because intrepid means brave and fearless in the face of danger or disaster. This word reflects the bravery and fearless demeanor of Emmett Till when his captors threatened to kill him if he did not surrender to their will. Even though he had been severely beaten and mutilated he did not surrender his will to his murders. He was not afraid of losing his life, even when it was most likely that he would be killed. Some may say they could not have endured the torture and pain and they would just have to kill them right on the spot. It was conditioned fear that kept black people in bondage for 250 years and another 100 years of involuntary servitude. The museum is named in honor of a brave and fearless boy named Emmett Till, who lost his life as a result of two evil white men in Tallahatchie County. The meaning of the name of the museum, ETHIC, is as follows:

Emmett   The first name of the 14-year-old boy who was murdered.

Till   A fourteen-year-old African American child from Chicago, who whistled at a Caucasian woman in a grocery store in Money, Mississippi. He was then brutally beaten, shot, and killed by two Caucasian men.

Historic   A tragic event in history that led to the Montgomery bus boycott. The boycott led to the Civil Rights Movement in the United States.

Intrepid   Never again will African Americans be fearful of taking a stand for justice. Never will our tongues be held. Never again will we let another race dominate us. Never again will we let this happen.

Center   A place where people can receive and learn information about an event that started a movement.

You are about to take a tour of one of the most unique museums in America that is comprised of a number of special exhibits. This museum is about more than the Emmett Till tragedy; it is also about the people and culture of the small rural town of Glendora, in Tallahatchie County, in the heart of the Mississippi Delta, one of the most economically depressed regions in the country. The museum exhibits include: artifacts used on plantations and by rural families; relics of Sonny Boy Williamson, II, the renowned king of the blues harmonica, and a native of Glendora; the King's Place Juke Joint, known as the "Caddilac" of Tallahatchie County; the Tree of Life; a Mississippi civil rights timeline; black veteran's memorial; and information and exhibits on the history and culture of the people of Glendora and Tallahatchie County.

We say that the Civil Rights Movement began here in Glendora, Mississippi because when Rosa Parks refused to give up her seat on the bus to a white man and refused to move to the back of the bus in Montgomery, Alabama, she later said that she thought about this kid in Mississippi, Emmett Till, who was brutally killed by two white men. That's why we say that the Emmett Till murder ignited the Civil Rights Movement.

Exhibit 1. History of Glendora and Tallahatchie County

Please step into the video room, have a seat, and learn about the history, trials, tribulations, and triumphs of the people of Glendora and Tallahatchie County. The video is about 10 minutes long. (after viewing video) Now, let's move to the first exhibit on the history and culture of Glendora. Glendora was established around plantation agriculture, logging, and timber processing, done mostly by black laborers. Settlers transported logs down river to be sawed and converted into timber in an area near the present-day site of Glendora. These loggers formed a settlement near Black Bayou. In 1883 a rail line was built and then a train depot. A post office and voting precinct were added and a charter was established and signed in March 1900 by William Gay, the first mayor. A total of 85 residents inhabited the new village.

Cotton, corn, rice, and soybeans were produced on small farms and large plantations. The agricultural work was done mostly by black laborers. Men, women and children worked in the fields for 12 hours a day or more, laboring hard under intense temperatures and physical working conditions for subsistence pay. Most of the large plantations operated as self-sustained communities with their own school, church, and homes. For the most part, there was strict racial segregation of blacks and whites on the plantations.

By the end of the American Civil War, blacks in Tallahatchie County found themselves emancipated from the bonds of slavery. The 13th Amendment to the Constitution granted blacks freedom from enslavement. The 14th Amendment granted Americans equal protection under the law; and the 15 Amendment granted Americans citizenship, including the right to vote. However, the problem was that in practice, these Amendments did not apply to blacks who were denied these rights. To prevent blacks from voting or being elected to public office, the "white man's party" sent army patrols to prevent blacks from voting and being elected to office. Blacks who opposed this force were murdered by armed gangs. Throughout the country white vigilantes, night riders, and gangs provoked riots and shot down blacks who resisted. Many blacks flooded the polls only to be turned away by a poll tax, constitutional tests, physical threats and intimidation, economic reprisals, and even lynches.

Black labor continued to provide a dominant economic, social, and political force in Glendora throughout the 1950s and 1960s. This period signaled the slow decline of the plantation system as plantation laborers were displaced by mechanized labor-saving machines that had created a "cotton kingdom." The civil rights movement gained momentum during this period with African Americans pushing for voter registration and equality of public facilities, and civil rights. Glendora was the first town in Tallahatchie County to elect an African American to a public office. Henry Reese was elected the first African American Mayor of Glendora in 1976 and Thomas A. Williams served on the Board of Aldermen. Blues singers created a "Mecca" of musical culture that continued to evolve. Glendora is the birthplace of Aleck "Rice" Miller, known as "Sonny Boy" Williams II, world renowned king of the blues harmonica.

Between 1940 and 1960, Jewish business owners dominated the economy of the town, before a series of fires destroyed most of the businesses. The remaining dilapidated buildings were sold or leased to African Americans. Robert Hilson purchased a substantial amount of the property and built King's Place, which consisted of a juke joint, café, auto mechanic shop, and apartments. Glendora became a thriving weekend and entertainment district earning the reputation as the "Las Vegas of the Plantations" in Tallahatchie County. Sonny Boy Williamson II, renowned blues singer and king of the blues harmonica, often performed at King's Place.

During those days, people would come from the surrounding plantations and farms for shopping, banking, entertainment, and business. However, over the years, several catastrophes hit the town, including the great fire that burned down most of the businesses, racial conflict created by racial desegregation of public schools, white flight and abandonment of the town by white businesses and politicians, a train derailment, and racial strife surrounding the Emmett Till murder and the ensuing trial of the defendants.

Today about 200 residents live in the town of Glendora. Glendora is still a poor town by national standards. The unemployment rate is 40% and about 40 percent of the people live below the poverty line. Most of the young and middle-aged people have migrated from the town in search of employment and a better quality of life in the cities. We, here in Glendora, have been called the people left behind. But there is a stone of hope for Glendora. As a part of that hope, this museum is a venture into cultural tourism to promote economic revitalization of the town. We are hopeful that the museum will draw many tourists to the town to learn about the Emmett Till tragedy, lessons learned from the past, and information about the history and culture of the people in this small hamlet in the heart of the Mississippi Delta. We are expecting visitors to come to Glendora to learn about how we live and survive, despite the wretched conditions and circumstances of the past. When the tourists come, they will bring much needed revenue to help in the economic revitalization of this town. We realize that this is only a piece of the puzzle for economic development and only time will tell if it will work.

Exhibit 2. Sonny Boy Williamson, II Sings the Blues "Don't Start Me Talking"

The Blues, as a musical genre, has its roots in the ritual music of the ancient Dogan people of the Mali Empire of West Africa Core elements of this style were transported from West African to America on slave ships where enslaved Africans moaned of the pain and horrific, dehumanizing conditions they suffered during the journey over the Atlantic Ocean to an unknown and uncertain destiny. In the plantation culture of the South, these songs evolved into unique musical expressions of pain, hardships, suffering, social relations, and protests that covered social, economic, political, and spiritual life. The music also included uplifting spiritual themes and expressions pertaining to pathways to freedom and liberation. Blues sentiments can be found in every form of music created by African Americans from slavery to liberation to social and political revolutions, and modern hip-hop.

Scores, perhaps hundreds of blues singers came out of the southern plantation culture of the South, and many of them were from the Mississippi Delta. Some of the most well-known blues artists from the Mississippi Delta were: Lead Belly; Charley Patton; Robert Johnson; David "Honeyboy" Edwards; Son House; Howlin Wolf; Elmore James; Muddy Waters; John Lee Hooker; B.B. King; and Sonny Boy Williamson, II. Sonny Boy Williamson II (1908-1965) was a native of Glendora. He was born on a plantation in Glendora, owned by Selwyn Jones, who was called to task by Mississippi Governor Earl Brewer for mistreatment of African Americans in 1915.

Sonny Boy Williamson II was born Aleck "Rice" Miller in Glendora, Mississippi on December 5, 1912 to Millie Ford and Jim Miller. The youngest and sole musician of 21 siblings, he became a childhood preacher and harmonica player known as "Reverend Blue" at the early age of six years old. Sonny Boy spent time at Parchman Penitentiary for allegedly stealing a mule. Escaping from prison, he assumed several identities as stage performer, including "Harmonica-blowing Slim," "Little Boy Blue," "Footsie," and "The Goat." In 1941, Sonny Boy and guitarist Robert Junior Lockwood co-hosted a 15-minute radio show broadcast, called "King Biscuit Time," on KFFA in Helena, Arkansas. This daily show, hosted by the legendary "Sunshine" Sonny Payne, became a favorite amongst blacks and whites and was the longest running broadcast of its kind in history. The sponsor, Max Moore, of the Interstate Grocery, found instant success by advertising King Biscuit Flour. This led to the creation of the "Sonny Boy Corn Meal Mix," a big seller and iconic brand for the band, becoming the first time blacks were included in the product advertisement business. King Biscuit Time was the longest running broadcast of its kind in history.

Sonny Boy was a colorful and charismatic performer who was perhaps the greatest and most renowned harmonica players ever born in the Mississippi Delta. He was known as "King of the Harmonica" and became famous for his two-toned tailored suits, bowler hat, umbrella, and satchel. His preferred harmonica was a 10-hole Holner Marine Band model. He was also a remarkable poetic composer of blues songs. His impressive musical legacy included a number of recordings, including: "Eyesight to the Blind," "Help Me," "Your Funeral and My Trial," "The Key," "Fattening Frogs for Snakes," "Nine Below Zero," "Mighty Long Time," "Unseeing Eye," "Don't Start Me Talkin" and "Keep It To Yourself." Most recorded for Trumpet records in Jackson, Mississippi and Chess/Checker Company of Chicago. He made many appearances at the King's Place Juke Joint, where I got a chance to see him in the latter part of his career.

During his career, Williamson teamed with such legendary artists as Robert Johnson (who they say he sold his soul to the devil and allegedly died in Williamson's arms), James, Muddy Waters, Robert Lockwood, Jr., B.B. King, Buddy Guy, Eric Clapton (recording his first guitar solo), Robert Jr. Lockwood (Johnson's stepson), harp legends and students James Cotton, Little Walter, Junior Parker, Junior Wells, Howlin' Wolf (Sonny Boy was married to his sister, Mary), Elmore James (joining him on the classic original "Dust My Broom"), and his King Biscuit Entertainers Pinetop Perkins, Joe Willie Perkins, Peck Curtis, Robert Jr. Lockwood, Dudlow Taylor, and the legendary "Sunshine" Sonny Payne.

During the 1960s, he became a popular celebrity in England, but in 1965, he came back to Glendora for a few weeks, where he stayed with his cousin, Willie James Stewart, and performed at Stewart's King's Place Juke Joint. It was at King's Place where I first saw one of his last performances when I was a young lad about eight years old. Sonny Boy was elected to the Blues Hall of Fame in the first year of balloting in 1980. On May 25, 1965, Sonny Boy Williamson II died from an apparent heart attack. He is buried in Tutwiler, Tallahatchie County, Mississippi.

Exhibit 3. The Veterans Memorial

Blacks have contributed to every aspect of American life, including service in the U.S. Military. Although proving themselves to be reputable soldiers, hatred against people of color permeated the military, as there was discrimination in pay, segregated units, unfair treatment, and by some eyewitness accounts, wrongful deaths. More than 185,000 African Americans served in the American Civil War (1861-1865), serving on both the Union and Confederate sides. By World War I, (1914-1918), there were more than 350,000 African American soldiers serving in segregated units. The first black U.S. combat units to fight in the Civil War in Mississippi dated back to 1863 at Ship Island (near Pascagoula, MS). The soldiers were members of the 2nd regiment of Louisiana Native Guards (Corps D'Afrique). More than 18,000 African Americans joined the Union Army and Navy regiments based in Mississippi. The Bureau of Colored Troops was established by the U.S. War Department to facilitate the process of recruiting black soldiers and was soon transformed into the United States Colored Troops (USCT). Although black military personnel fought in the most significant battles, many were denied proper recognition of the braveness and heroic contributions of all black military personnel. These soldiers increased their involvement in protests against racial injustices on the home front and abroad.

By World War II (1941-1945), the number of blacks serving in the military reached nearly one million. In spite of all indications that black soldiers could perform military tasks on the same level as whites, they remained segregated. Pressure heightened to integrate the U.S. military. Despite orders from President Harry Truman in 1948, blacks were still kept in separate units during most of the Korean War, and it was not until the Vietnam War that blacks fully participated in the war alongside their white military counterparts. Regardless of their sacrificial commitment and service, upon returning home to the U.S., black soldiers were severely mistreated and encountered an unjust, unequal, segregated, and highly racist environment.

The town of Glendora recognizes the hard working and dedicated service of its own native U.S. Army Staff Sergeant, Leslie Daryel Johnson. Sergeant Johnson joined the Army in 1998 and served in Kosovo, Thailand, and two tours in Iraq, proudly wearing his uniform. In executing his missions, he received letters of commendation, metals and awards for outstanding service and leadership as a non-commissioned officer (NCO), which is often referred to as the "backbone" of the armed services. Sergeant Johnson further expanded his military training, pursuing a degree in Nursing.

Robert Grayson, served 22 years in the Armed Forces with a tour in Vietnam. He received a Purple Heart, a Bronze Star, and a Silver Star for his service in Vietnam. He served as the mayor of Tutwiler for 16 years. Jerome G. Little served in the Marine Corp from 1974 to 1977. After serving his country, he returned to Tallahatchie and fought for water rights for his family and community in the Goose-Pond sub-division in Webb, Mississippi; he was part of the "Magnificent Seven," a group of black men who sued Tallahatchie County several times in order to hold political positions. These men held several countywide boycotts of stores and schools in cooperation with the county and state NAACP. In 1994, Jerome Little became the first African American to serve on the County Board of Supervisors. In 1996, he was elected vice-president of the Board, and in 2000 he was elected president. In 2006, he helped form the Emmett Till Memorial Commission.

Exhibit 4. Plantation Commissaries and General Stores

Following the Civil War, slavery on plantations shifted to plantation laborers, tenant farmers, or sharecroppers. Plantation commissaries were established by plantation owners to warehouse supplies for laborers and families who lived and worked on the plantation. Commissaries were stocked with commodities for daily survival, including salt, coffee, flour, seeds, medicines, clothing, and household goods. In the early 20th century, many plantation owners began using their commissaries like general stores where sharecroppers throughout the region could obtain needed supplies. Independent general stores also emerged to compete with or complement plantation commissaries. Chinese merchants were a dominant force in this trend, as were poor whites looking for a way to advance above the constraints and debt traps faced by blacks. General stores were also social places where local residents could gather to share news and information, and lighten the load of their daily burdens through games, music, and the like. Bryant's Grocery and Meat Market in Money, Mississippi was one of the few stores in the area that would sell provisions to black sharecroppers and community children and youth.

Exhibit 5. King's Place

"For Mississippi at that time, King's Place wasn't a typical juke joint. It was a jazzy place with live music, food, and lots of activities." – Robert Walker

Juke joints in the Mississippi Delta usually sprang up in shanty quarters where cotton pickers and sharecroppers gathered to find a release from their day-to-day troubles without fear of racial intimidation or punishment. Reverberating from the walls were songs of complaint, hardship, lamentations, love relationships, companionship, celebration, and tragedy. King's Place emerged in Glendora in the 1940s after Robert Hilson acquired the property for development. Guest from nearby towns and villages were attracted to the juke joint for some rustic entertainment to hear some "down home blues" for 25 cents admission, or to eat some "soul food" from the café such as stews, hamburgers, pork chops, and pigs feet. Igniting the spirit of the Blues for more than four decades, King's Place contributed to the thriving entertainment district in Glendora, offering live music, dancing, drinking, pool, table games, and gambling. During his final sojourn to the Mississippi Delta before his death, Sonny Boy Williamson, II performed a dynamic "farewell" set at King's Place. Contributing to its long-term success, King's Place had steady ownership with Willie James Stewart, nephew of Sonny Boy Williamson, II, owning it well into the 1980s. Although other attempts were made to take it over, many suspected that King's Place had already established its "royal impact" among juke joints in the Delta.

Exhibit 6. The Send Off

This is the "Send Off" exhibit which is very significant because before Emmett Till left Chicago his mother gave him his father's ring to remember her by. Till was in such a hurry to come to Mississippi to visit his relatives, he forgot to kiss his mother goodbye. His mother called him back and said, "haven't gotten a goodbye kiss from you; how will I know I will see you again?" And his mother gave him a signet ring that she had received at the death of his father that had his father's initials L.T. engraved on it. Till removed his watch from his wrist and gave it to his mother, saying "I won't need this where I am going," as if he knew he would not be coming back to Chicago, but going to an eternal home. Who could have guessed that this would be an important event before his death and the beginning of the Civil Rights Movement. Moses Wright and his wife and their three children were in the house when Milam and Bryant came to take Till.

Exhibit 7. Bryant's Store

Roy and Carolyn Bryant ran a small grocery, Bryant's Grocery & Meat Market, that sold provisions to black sharecroppers and their children. The store was located at one end of the main street in the tiny town of Money, the heart of the cotton-growing Mississippi Delta. They had two sons and lived in two small rooms in the back of the store. To earn extra cash, Roy worked as a trucker with his half-brother J.W. Milam, an imposing man of six feet two inches, weighing 235 pounds. Milam prided himself on knowing how to "handle" blacks. He had served in World War II and received combat metals. This is the place where Emmett Till and some of his cousins stopped to buy candy on the fateful Saturday afternoon August 24, 1955, when young Till playfully whistled at Carolyn Bryant, the clerk in the store and wife of Roy Bryant, that led to the unforgettable nightmare involving the abduction and murder of Till by Bryant and his half-brother, J. W. Milam.

Exhibit 8. The Crime

On August 28, 1955, at about 2:30 a.m. Roy Bryant, J.W. Milam, and at least one other person went to the house of Emmett Till's great uncle, Moses Wright, a preacher and sharecropper. Barging in with a .45 caliber gun and a 5-cell flashlight they told Moses Wright that they had "come for that boy from Chicago who had done that smart talk at Money." Moses Wright and his wife, Elizabeth pleaded with the men to leave Emmett alone. "He's only 14, he's from the North. Why not give the boy a whipping, and leave it at that?" Elizabeth Wright offered money to the intruders, but they ordered her to go back to bed. The men refused and ordered Moses to lead them throughout his home with flashlights to find the bed where Emmett was sleeping. They woke him up and ordered him to get dressed. Emmett complied with the order and put on his clothes and "walked out of the house without saying another word." Milam turned to Moses and threatened him saying, "How old are you, preacher?" Wright said that he was sixty-four. "If you make trouble, you'll never live to be sixty-five." Wright and other family members waited for hours, hoping and praying that the men would only put a scarring into Emmett, and then return him relatively unscathed. When rumors swept over Tallahatchie County that Emmett had been killed, despite threats, Moses Wright drove to nearby Greenwood and told the sheriff about two men coming to his home and abducting Emmett.

The crimes committed by J.W. Milam and Roy Bryant in the Emmett Till case included the following: kidnapping with a deadly weapon (.45 caliber pistol); aggravated assault and battery by torture (forcibly constrained Till for hours on the back of a pick-up truck during a near 200 mile excursion through the Delta and severely beating Till); lynching with a gin fan and barbed wire; gunshot through the head; concealing evidence of a felony by dumping the body into the river; drowning to hide the evidence; first degree murder; and destroying evidence of a felony (burning of Emmett Till clothes). The criminal weapons that served as evidence in the kidnapping and murder were a .45 caliber revolver; 5-cell flashlight; military knife; 75 pound gin fan; and barbed wire. Another possible crime was forcing employees or loyal subjects to participate in a felony. In the case of the latter, Mrs. Till-Mobley and others believed that Milam and Bryant ordered their subjects to participant in the kidnapping, beating, murder, and disposal of the body. Although Milam and Bryant, later confessed to killing Emmett Till, many believed that their confession was not fully truthful because they did not want to reveal everyone who was involved in the kidnapping and murder.

Exhibit 9. The Search for Emmett

Moses and Elizabeth Wright got word to Emmett's mother in Chicago that her son was missing. The family and a local sheriff attempted to look for him by searching along the riverbanks and under bridges, "where black folks always look when something like this happens," as Moses would recall. Emmett Till's body was found in the Tallahatchie River, a heavy gin fan tied around his neck with barbed wire. Roy Bryant and J.W. Milam were arrested and brought to trial.

Exhibit 10. Glendora Cotton Gin

This building was once a thriving cotton gin that ginned cotton that was harvested from surrounding plantations. The gin was owned and operated by Roy Bryant and J. W. Milam, who employed African American workers to perform much of the manual labor required to operate the gin. This gin was the location where the 75 pound gin fan was retrieved by Milam and Roy Bryant that they tied with barbed wire around the neck of Emmett Till before his body was thrown off the Black Bayou Bridge into the bayou in Glendora.

Exhibit 11. Sheridan's Barn

This is the place where Emmett Till was taken and severely beaten. The barn was owned by the Sheridan Plantation, which was located in Sunflower County. Some believe that this is where Till died from the beating and wounds inflicted on him by his kidnappers, J.W. Milam and Bryant, and possibly other unknown persons, before his body was taken to Glendora and dumped into the bayou off of the Black Bayou Bridge.

Exhibit 12. The Black Bayou Bridge

According to an eyewitness account, after Emmett Till was murdered, his body was actually thrown off the Black Bayou Bridge in Glendora rather than in the Tallahatchie River, as the news media reported. Some may ask what difference does it make? Well it made a lot of difference in how the case was investigated, how evidence was collected, interrogation of witnesses near the crime scene, verification of local folklore, and to ensure historical accuracy, correct identification, and preservation of the event. Why would a historic marker be placed on the Tallahatchie River Bridge, when Emmett Till's body was actually thrown off the Black Bayou Bridge? In this way, the Town of Glendora is not recognized as the place, where not only the murder was conceived, but where Till's body was actually dumped in order to get rid of the evidence. My father said that Emmett Till's body was thrown off the Black Bayou Bridge. He would have known because I believe he was there to witness it. The Black Bayou drops into the Tallahatchie River right around the corner from Glendora, so it is logical that the body could have washed down the Black Bayou into the mouth of the Tallahatchie River where it was found.

There were other accounts about the murder of Emmett Till that did not surface until well after the trial was over because of only one news reporter, James Hicks, who worked for the black news wire service, the National Negro Publishers Association. Hicks actually went into the black community to conduct research and question people about the Emmett Till murder. A friend of mine, who was a young boy at the time, told me that on the Sunday morning after the abduction and murder of Emmett Till, he saw Till's body in the back of J.W. Milam's truck. He said that J.W. Milam had called his father over to look at the body, and stated that Milam said, "Come here let me show you something that we do to niggers when they get all smart." And he raised the tarp on the truck. The kid said that he ran over and peeped under the tarp and saw Emmett Till's severely beaten body. He said that his father told him not to ever say anything about what he saw, and if he did, it would cause them to be killed as well. And that's what he feared all of his life without talking about it. However, he did talk to the FBI later and gave his account of the suffering, trauma, and nightmares he went through. He said he also had nightmares of his father dragging him away from the truck so fast to get him away from the scene. He said he still has nightmares from seeing Till's body. He said he saw my father [Henry Lee Loggins] the next morning just prior to the disposing of Till's body (Excerpts from DRCI, Mississippi Valley State University and Delta Media Project).

Now the Black Bayou Bridge has been closed. I think they closed it in an effort to kill the town. Before the bridge was closed, Glendora was a thriving town. This was the main thoroughfare to Glendora. On a given weekend, as many as a thousand people would convene in Glendora to visit the town, especially to shop and socialize at the King's Place Juke Joint. People would come from surrounding towns, such as Greenwood, Grenada, Cleveland, Ruleville, Minter City, Phillips, and Charleston. I owned several businesses then, and they were thriving. A new road was built later that by-passed Glendora, and since that time the town has slowly deteriorated. However, we are going to clean it up and open it up for tourism, as a historic site with one of the true stories about the Emmett Till murder (Excerpts from DRCI, Mississippi Valley State University & Delta Media Project).

Exhibit 13. River Site

This is the site where Till's body was removed from the river. It was then taken to Greenwood, Mississippi. The body was sent back to Money, Mississippi for burial. Via a phone call from Till's mother, "not to bury her son," the body was then taken back to Greenwood. The body was then sent to Tutwiler, Mississippi for final preparation to be sent to Chicago, Illinois.

Exhibit 14. The Tree of Life

We put together the "Tree of Life" exhibit to reflect all of the families and witnesses involved in the Emmett Till murder case: Simeon Wright, Emmet Till's cousin, who was in bed with Emmet Till before Till was abducted and murdered. Reverend Wheeler Parker, who travelled with Emmett Till from Chicago to Moses Wright's house, on Dark Fear Road, just outside of Money, Mississippi in Leflore County; Willie Reed, who said he heard the beating of Emmet Till in the Sheridan barn in Sunflower County; and Reverend Moses Wright, Emmett Till's great uncle, who was the first African American in Mississippi to testify against a white person, by standing up in the courtroom and pointing to Milam and Bryant as the men who came to his house around 2:30 a.m. in the morning and abducted Emmett Till.

Exhibit 15. The Trial

Mississippi may as well burn all its law books and close its courts
if the maximum penalty of the law cannot be
secured in this heinous crime. Editorial,
Clarksdale Press Register, September 1955.
They are calling this a lynching in some places outside of Mississippi.
Well, it wasn't. But it may well become a lynching post-facto,
if the courts in Mississippi are unable to accomplish justice in this matter.
And if that happens, we will deserve the criticism we get.
Delta Democrat-Times, September 6, 1955.
You kill sixteen jigs, and what do you git?
A Freestate Jury that'll always acquit;
Saint Peter don't you call Emmett, cause he can't go,
he owes his soul to Bryant's sto.

Chorus from popular song among Tallahatchie County teenagers, following the acquittal (Whitaker, Hugh Stephen. *A Case Study in Southern Justice: The Emmett Till Case.* Master's Thesis, University of Florida, 1963, p. 172).

Judge Curtis Swango presided over the notorious trial of J.W. Milam and Roy Bryant, who were charged with kidnapping and murder of Emmett Till. Milam and Bryant appeared before the grand jury on September 5, 1955. Statements were issued by Leflore County Sheriff, George Smith, Deputy John Ed Cothran, Tallahatchie County Sheriff H.C. Strider, and Deputy Garland Melton. The most significant testimony of the day came from the Tallahatchie County sheriff, that the body pulled from the river had not been satisfactorily identified as Emmett Till's. Rumors were already circulating in Sumner about the NAACP's involvement and the probability that the murder accusation had been planned by the organization. Strider claimed that the body could not be positively identified, that the ring on his finger had been planted there, and that Emmett Till was surely still alive in Chicago. This theory would be the basis for the defense's argument in court. The conspiracy theory was outrageous, but the possibility that the NAACP had orchestrated things was not out of the question, from the mindset of white southerners.

At the end of the hearings on September 6, the grand jury indicted Milam and Bryant on charges of kidnapping and murder, though the prosecuting attorney claimed he did not seek the death penalty. Their arraignment took place later that afternoon, when Seventeenth Judicial District Judge Curtis Swango heard their "not guilty" plea.

The atmosphere in Sumner was very tense. Sumner was being put on display as a typical rural southern town where such horrendous crimes as this one could be committed, although Sumner was not where the murder was committed. Milam was from Glendora, a Tallahatchie County town roughly twenty miles from Sumner and Bryant was from Money, where Till was abducted, in Leflore County. Because the body surfaced on the Tallahatchie County riverbank, the county seat was entitled to take the case. The residents of Sumner resented being labeled as the area where the murder occurred and feared that the trial coverage might turn into a "Roman Holiday" spectacle (William M. Simpson, Reflections on a Murder: The Emmett Till Case, 1981, p. 87). When asked several times by an interviewer in front of a news camera whether he thought the defendants should be convicted, one young black man's steady reply was, "I really don't know, sir" (Stanley Nelson, *"The Murder of Emmett Till."* American Experience, Public Broadcasting Service, 2003, p. 11).

At the trial, members of the defense team were J.J. Breland and his partner John W. Whitten, Jr., J.W. Kellum, R. Harvey Henderson, and C. Sidney Carlton. Members of the prosecution were District Attorney Gerald Chatham, Tallahatchie County Prosecutor Hamilton Caldwell, and Special Assistant Attorney General B. Smith.

The atmosphere in the courtroom and in the communities surrounding the trial was unsettling. Reporters especially were looked upon with contempt and the entire community was preoccupied with the commotion created by the murder and trial. In an interview, Sumner resident Betty Pearson stated that,

> We had a plantation out from Webb, Rainbow Plantation, so that's where I was…The four nights that [the press] were here, we had five or six guys out there every night and it was really interesting because of the conversation we had after supper. Everybody talked about what happened. That

was the fun part of it (*"Covering a Mississippi Murder Trial—The Emmett Till Lynching,"* p. 98, publication information unavailable).

Pearson also provided the following description of Sheriff Clarence Strider of Tallahatchie County:

> He was this fat sheriff, Sheriff Strider, who had on pants with suspenders. He was fat, and he looked like a picture out of a movie, like a southern sheriff. He played the part well. He [Sheriff Strider] liked to demonstrate his friendliness with Negro reporters covering the trial by greeting them each day with: "Good morning niggers." Meanwhile the defendants sat with their families behind the railing in the courtroom, and one of [Milam's children] played a solitary game, waving his toy water pistol at a sheriff and shouting boom! boom! boom! Another time, little Harvey Milam amused himself by slipping a rope around his brother's neck and tugging at it (*Covering a Mississippi Murder Trial—The Emmett Till Lynching,* p. 98, publication information unavailable).

The first day of the trial was dedicated entirely to the selection of the jury. Milam and Bryant were not well known by Tallahatchie residents and had their reputations to rely on. The prosecution hoped for jurors from the east side of the county, the hill country, under the incorrect assumption that those men were father from Milam and Bryant and were, therefore, less likely to be friends of theirs.

On September 8, 1955, on the motion of the State Circuit Court, Judge Swango ordered a special venire of 120 men to be drawn from the jury boxes, in open court, on September 12. The special venire gave the state a choice to get half of the jurors from the east side of the county, far from the homes of the accused. (Whitaker, Hugh Stephen. *A Case Study in Southern Justice: The Emmett Till Case.* Master's Thesis, University of Florida, 1963, p. 142).

Several fallacies in the selection of the jurors were noted by Huge Whitaker:

First, except for a few close friends, people who knew Milam and Bryant disliked them and were afraid of them…Second, the prosecutors failed to note the distinct differences which have always existed between the hills and the delta. Nearly all of beat 1 and most of Beat 2 and 13 are in the hills; here most white farmers were in competition with negroes, and did not feel the intense noblesse oblige that was common to many of the large landowners of the delta. Men from the east side of the county were also deputized by Sheriff Strider, patrolling the streets, brandishing the weapons on their hips, and upsetting the Sumner residents even more (Whitaker, Hugh Stephen. *A Case Study in Southern Justice: The Emmett Till Case.* Master's Thesis, University of Florida, 1963, p. 155).

Exhibit 16. Moses Wright Standing Up for Justice

During the trial, Moses Wright defied all historical odds. When asked if he could identify the man who came to his home with the gun, he replied, "Yes sir"! He then stood up in open court and pointed his finger at J.W. Milam and emphatically stated with the simple words, "There he is" and for clarity, he shifted his unshaken finger toward Roy Bryant and said "and there is Mr. Bryant." This moment went down in history as perhaps the first time a black man stood up in an open Southern court, accused a white man of a crime—and lived!! After the September murder trial, Moses Wright fled to Chicago to join his wife. He returned to Greenwood in November to testify at the grand jury hearing on Milam and Bryant's kidnapping charges. When the grand jury refused to return an indictment, Wright left for Chicago and never returned to Mississippi again.

On Thursday, Mamie Till-Mobley took the stand, certain that she could identify her only child's body. Also, on the roster was another blow to the defense's argument: surprise witness Willie Reed, who had seen and heard the beatings at Leslie Milam's plantation. The defense relied on the testimonies of Carolyn Bryant, Dr. L.B. Otken, and Dr. H.D. Malone. Mrs. Bryant recalled the incident in the store, claiming that Till had not only touched her but handled her roughly, saying inappropriate things until she managed to escape his grasp. Her testimony was dismissed by Swango, however, because it did not relate directly to the case in question.

Friday brought six character witnesses to the courtroom, and then the focus moved on to the prosecution and defense's summations. John W. Whitten, Jr., in defense of Milam and Bryant, stated that "every last Anglo Saxon one of you has the courage to set these men free," and warned that the jurors forefathers would "turn over in their graves" if these boys were convicted on such evidence as this.

Hugh Whitaker stated that,

> Meanwhile, a desperate but unhopeful Gerald Chatham said, They murdered that boy, and to hide that dastardly, cowardly act, they tied barbed wire to his neck and to a heavy gin fan and dumped him in the river for the turtles and the fish. He said the defendants were dripping with the blood of Emmett Till. (Whitaker, Hugh Stephen. *A Case Study in Southern Justice: The Emmett Till Case.* Master's Thesis, University of Florida, 1963, p. 153).

Exhibit 17. Robert's Temple Church of God In Christ

Emmett Till's body was placed on display at Roberts Temple Church of God In Christ on the South Side of Chicago. His mother decided to have an open-casket funeral to let the world see the brutal nature in which her son had been killed. The casket had a plate of glass covering Emmett Till's upper body, assuring that his severely mutilated and disfigured face was fully visible. On a Sunday afternoon, more than 50,000 Chicagoans and people from around the country passed through the church to view the body and witness what had been done to one of their own. Families brought their children with them, and many fainted and had to be assisted out of the building (Stanley Nelson, *"The Murder of Emmett Till."* American Experience, Public Broadcasting Service, 2003, p. 6).

Exhibit 18. The Place of Rest

After the funeral at Roberts Temple Church of God In Christ, Emmett Till's body was laid to rest in the Burr Oak Cemetery in Chicago. The headstone on his grave was engraved with the words: EMMETT L. TILL, In Loving Memory, July 25, 1941 to August 28, 1955. The headstone was adorned with a Medallion, with an inset picture of Till.

Exhibit 19. Lasting Impressions – The Freedom Quilt

The freedom quilt is a composition of symbols, images, and expressions woven into fabric that provides a pictorial history of freedom. The artistic renderings are centered around historical images of Emmett Till.

Exhibit 20. Timeline of the Emmett Till Tragedy and The Murder Trial

May

7   The Reverend George Lee, a grocery store owner and NAACP field worker in Belzoni, Mississippi, is shot and killed at point blank range while driving in his car after trying to vote. A few weeks later in Brookhaven, Mississippi, Lamar Smith, another black man, is shot and killed in front of the county courthouse, in broad daylight and witnesses, after casting his ballot. Both victims had been active in voter registration drives. No one was arrested in connection with with either case.

August

19   A day before her son is to leave for a summer stay with family in Mississippi, Mamie Till gives Emmett the ring once owned by his father, Louis Till. It is inscribed with the initials L.T.

20   Mamie Till rushes her son Emmett to the 63rd Street station in Chicago to catch the southbound train to Money, Mississippi.

21   Emmett Till arrives in Money, Mississippi and goes to stay at the home of his great uncle Moses Wright and his great aunt Elizabeth Wright.

24   Emmett joins a group of teenagers, seven boys and one girl, to go to Bryant's Grocery and Meat Market for refreshments to cool off after a long day of picking cotton in the hot sun. Bryant's Grocery, owned and supplied candy to a primarily black clientele of sharecroppers and their children. Emmett goes into the store to buy bubble gum. Some of the kids outside the store will later say they heard Emmett whistle at Carolyn Bryant, wife of Roy Bryant.

28   About 2:30 a.m., Roy Bryant, Carolyn's husband, and his half-brother, J.W. Milam, kidnap Emmett Till from Moses Wright's home. They will later describe brutally beating him, taking him to the edge of the Tallahatchie River, shooting him in the head, fastening a large metal fan used for ginning cotton to his neck with barbed wire, and pushing the body into the river.

29   J.W. Milam and Roy Bryant are arrested on kidnapping charges in Leflore County in connection with Till's disappearance. They are jailed in Greenwood, Mississippi and held without bond.

31   Three days later, Emmett Till's decomposed corpse is pulled from the Tallahatchie River. Moses Wright identifies the body from a ring with the initials L.T.

September

1   Mississippi Governor, Hugh White, orders local officials to "fully prosecute" Milam and Bryant in the Till case.

2   In Chicago, Mamie Till arrives at the Illinois Central Terminal to receive Emmett's casket. She is surrounded by family and photographers who snap her photo, collapsing in grief at the sight of the casket. The body is taken to the A.A. Rayner & Sons Funeral Home. The Jackson (Mississippi) Daily news describes the "brutal, senseless crime" but complains that the NAACP is working "to arouse hatred and fear" by calling Till's murder a lynching. In Belgium, the newspaper le Drapeau Rouge (The Red Flag), publishes a brief article entitled: "Racism in the USA: A young black is lynched in Mississippi."

3   Emmett Till's body is taken to Chicago's Roberts Temple Church of God In Christ for viewing and funeral services. Emmett's mother decides to have an open casket funeral. Thousands of Chicagoans wait in line to see Emmett's brutally beaten body.

6   Emmett Till is buried at Burr Oak Cemetery. The same day, a grand jury in Mississippi indicts Milam and Bryant for the kidnapping and murder of Emmett Till. They both plead innocent. They will be held in jail until the start of the trial.

15   Till's mutilated corpse was published by Jet Magazine, shocking and outraging African Americans from coast to coast.

17   The black newspaper, The Chicago Defender, publishes photographs of Till's corpse.

19   The kidnapping and murder trial of J.W. Milam and Roy Bryant opens in Sumner, Mississippi, the county seat of Tallahatchie County. Jury selection begins, and with blacks and white women banned from serving on the all-white, 12-man jury made up of nine farmers, two carpenters, and one insurance agent. Mamie Till Bradley departs from Chicago's Midway Airport to attend the trial.

20   Judge Curtis Swango recesses the court to allow more witnesses to be found. It is the first time in Mississippi history that local law enforcement, local NAACP leaders, and black and white reporters team up to locate sharecroppers who saw Milam's truck, and the French daily newspaper Le Monde runs an article reporting that the American public is following the Till case "with passionate attention."

21   Moses Wright, Emmett Till's great uncle, does the unthinkable – he accuses two white men in open court. While on the witness stand, he stands up and points his finger at Milam and Bryant, and accuses them of coming to his house and kidnapping Emmett.

23   Milam and Bryant are acquitted of murdering Emmett Till
      after the jury deliberates only 67 minutes. One juror tells a
      reporter that they wouldn't have taken so long if they hadn't
      stopped to drink pop. Roy Bryant and J.W. Milam stand
      before photographers, light up cigars, and kiss their wives
      in celebration of the not guilty verdict. Moses Wright and
      another poor black Mississippian who testified, Willie Reed,
      leave Mississippi and are smuggled to Chicago. Once there,
      Reed collapses and suffers a nervous breakdown.

26   In Belgium, two left-wing newspapers publish articles on the
      acquittal. Le People, the daily Belgian Socialist newspaper,
      calls the acquittal "a judicial scandal in the United States."
      Le Drapeau Rouge publishes "Killing a black person isn't a
      crime in the home of the Yankees: the white killers of young
      Emmett Till are acquitted!" In France, L'Aurore newspaper
      publishes: "The Scandalous Acquittal in Sumner" and the daily
      newspaper Le Figaro adds: "The Shame of the Sumner Jury."

27   The French daily newspaper Le Monde runs an article: "The
      Sumner Trial Marks, Perhaps, an Opening of Consciousness."

28   In Germany, the newspaper Freies Volk publishes: "The Life
      of a Negro Isn't Worth a Whistle." In France, the French
      Communist Party newspaper L'Humanite writes: "After the
      Mockery of Justice in Mississippi: Emotion in Parish."

30   Milam and Bryant are released on bond. Kidnapping charges
      are pending.

October

15   The Memphis Commercial Appeal publishes an article
      reporting that Louis Till was executed by the U.S. Army
      in Italy in 1945 for raping two Italian women and killing a
      third. Mississippi Senator James O. Eastland has leaked the
      information to the press.

22   The American Jewish Committee in New York releases
      a report urging Congress to bolster Federal civil rights
      legislation in light of the Till case. Their report included
      quotes from newspapers in six European countries expressing
      shock and outrage after the Till verdict.

November

9   Returning to Mississippi one last time, Moses Wright and Willie Reed testify before a Leflore County grand jury in Greenwood, Mississippi. The grand jury refuses to indict Milam and Bryant for kidnapping. The two white men go free.

December

5   One hundred days after Emmett Till's murder, Rosa Parks refuses to give up her seat on a city bus, launching the Montgomery, Alabama bus boycott and the Civil Rights Movement. The boycott will last 381 days.

January

22   Look Magazine publishes an article written by Alabama journalist William Bradford Huie, entitled "The Shocking Story of Approved Killing in Mississippi." Huie has offered Roy Bryant and J.W. Milam $4,000 to tell how they killed Emmett Till. Milam speaks for the record.

24   William Bradford Huie writes another article for Look Magazine, "What Happened to the Emmett Till Killers?" Huie writes that "Milam does not regret the killing, though it has brought him nothing but trouble." Blacks have stopped frequenting stores owned by the Milam and Bryant families and put them out of business. Bryant takes up welding for income, and both men are ostracized by the white community.

April
25
Three days before his scheduled trial, Mack Charles Parker, a 23-year-old African American truck driver, is lynched by a hooded mob of white men in Popoularville, Mississippi. Parker has been accused of raping a pregnant white woman and was being held in a local jail. The mob takes him from his cell, beats him, takes him to a bridge, shoots and kills him, then weighs his body down with chains and dumps him in the river. Many people know the identity of the killers, but the community closes ranks and refuses to talk. Echoing the Till case, the FBI will investigate and identify at least 10 men involved, but the U.S. Department of Justice will rule there are no federal grounds to make an arrest and press charges. Two grand juries — one county and one federal — will adjourn without indictments.

December 31, 1980, J.W. Milam dies in Mississippi of cancer, at age of 61.

September 1, 1994, Roy Bryant dies in Mississippi of cancer, at age of 63.

January 6, 2003, Mamie Till Mobley dies of heart failure, at age 81. Her death comes just two weeks before "The Murder of Emmett Till" is to premiere nationally on PBS.

CHAPTER 14

MOTHER MAMIE MOBLEY
AND WOMEN IN THE CIVIL RIGHTS MOVEMENT

A FRICAN AMERICAN WOMEN played a key role in the American Civil Rights Movement. Without their struggle for freedom and justice, it would not have been possible for Americans to achieve racial justice. However, African American women were not given the necessary credit that they deserved. Some of the most well-known women who played a major role in the Civil Rights movement in the State of Mississippi and the South are presented in the following section.

Mamie Carthan Till-Mobley, the mother of Emmett Till, was born on November 23, 1921 in a small town near Webb, Mississippi. She was the only child of John and Alma Carthan, and her family moved to Argo, Illinois, near Chicago when she was a toddler. Mamie was the first black "A" honor student and the fourth black student to graduate from the predominantly white Argo Community High School. She graduated from Chicago Teacher's College in 1956 and obtained a master's degree in administration from Loyola University, Chicago, in 1976. She taught special education in Chicago elementary schools. In 1955, Mrs. Till was thrusted into

American history when her only child, Emmett Louis Till, was brutally murdered near Sumner, Mississippi on August 28, 1955, ironically, two miles from her birthplace. Horrified by the mutilation of her son's body, Mamie made a stunning decision that Emmett would have an open-casket funeral. She stated, "I want the world to see what they did to my baby." Approximately 50,000 people viewed Emmett's Corpse in Chicago. Thousands of letters protesting the not guilty verdict of the two white men who murdered Till poured into the White House. Mamie took her fight to the people, giving speeches to overflowing crowds across the country, which galvanized the Civil Rights Movement. Membership in the NAACP soared. Mamie Till-Mobley was buried at Burr Oak Cemetery, the same cemetery where her son was buried. Her grave marker was inscribed with these words: "Her Pain United A Nation; Mamie Till-Mobley 1921-2003; Mamie Till-Mobley, the mother of the slain Emmett Louis Till, Jr. and the wife of the late Gennie Mobley, Jr.; Following the untimely death of her son, Emmett, on August 28, 1955. Mamie founded the Emmett Till Foundation, a nonprofit organization dedicated to perpetuating the memory of Emmett, whose brutal murder and the acquittal of his confessed kidnappers became the impetus for the Civil Rights Movement" (Women had key roles in the civil rights movement," msnbc.com).

Fannie Lou Hamer is known as the lady who made the famous expression "I am sick and tired of being sick and tired," in regard to the struggle to gain civil rights in Mississippi. She was born, October 6, 1917 in Montgomery County, Mississippi. She was beaten and jailed in Winona, Mississippi for attempting to register to vote. While she was traveling on a bus on June 3, 1963, state law enforcement officers in Winona, Mississippi took Hamer and fellow activists to Montgomery County jail where they were severely beaten. She testified that she was beaten until her "body was hard." She suffered a blood clot, severe damage to her kidney, and required a month to recover from the assault. As an instrumental figure in the struggle for civil rights, Hamer co-founded the Mississippi Freedom Democratic Party (MFDP). In 1964, the MFDP challenged the all-white Mississippi delegation to the Democratic National Convention. Hamer spoke to the Credentials Committee members in a televised proceeding that reached millions of viewers. She told the committee how African Americans in many states across the country were prevented from voting through illegal tests, taxes, and intimidation tactics. As a result of her speech, two delegates of the MFDP were permitted to speak at the convention and the other members were seated as honorable guests (Women had key roles in the civil rights movement," msnbc.com).

Rosa Parks is often referred to as the "Mother of the Civil Rights Movement." She was an African American activist that sparked the mass Bus Boycott movement in Montgomery, Alabama. She stated, that she "thought of Emmett Till and I couldn't go back…I am so thankful for the bravery and courage Mamie demonstrated when she shared her only child with the world. The memory of Emmett's death caused many people to participate in the cry for justice and equal rights, including myself" (Rosa Parks Biography: Standing Up for Freedom, Academy of Achievement, Washington, D.C.).

Jo Ann Robinson was a civil rights activist and educator in Montgomery, Alabama, who helped Rosa Parks fight for the racial justice in 1955. Prior to this incidence, in 1949, she suffered a humiliating experience when the bus driver ordered her to get off the bus for having sat in the fifth row. She was elected president of the Women's Political Council in 1950 and made racial desegregation of the city buses one of the priorities of the organization. She worked with Rosa Parks in organizing the boycott of buses in Montgomery (http:www.buzzle.com/articles/African-american-in-civil-rights-movement.html).

Diane Nash was a civil rights activist and one of the founders of the Student Non-Violent Coordinating Committee (SNCC) in April of 1960. She participated in the sit-in movement to desegregate lunch counters in 1960 in Nashville, TN. Although she was four-months pregnant, she was sentenced to two years in prison for teaching nonviolent tactics to children in Jackson, Mississippi (Women had key roles in the civil rights movement," msnbc.com).

Ella Josephine Baker was one of the first African American civil and human rights activists in the 1930s. She was a longtime leader in the Southern Christian Leadership Conference and a charismatic labor organizer, who mentored young civil rights leaders, including Rosa Parks and Diane Nash (Women had key roles in the civil rights movement," msnbc.com).

Endesha Ida Mae Holland was born in 1944 into abject poverty in Greenwood, Mississippi. She experienced extreme racism, and had few options to change her life. She was jailed numerous times for protesting with the SNCC movement. One of her protest trips was held at the state penitentiary with other civil rights activists, where she was imprisoned for 33 days. She went on to achieve her B.A. degree from the University of Minnesota, and her doctorate. She wrote a stage play entitled "From the Mississippi Delta." and became a tenured professor in American Studies at the State University of New York at Buffalo. She went on to teach at the University of Southern California where she retired in 2003 (www.usc.edu/ uscnews/ stories/12006.html).

Victoria Jackson Gray Adams, a native of Hattiesburg, Mississippi, and a key leader in the Civil Right Movement, helped Mississippi blacks win their civil rights in the 1960s. She was the first woman to seek a seat in the United States Senate from Mississippi. In July 1964, she announced that she and others from the tiny Mississippi Freedom Democratic Party would challenge the power of segregationist politician, Senator John Stennis, who represented her state. She stated that the time had come to pay attention "to the Negro in Mississippi, who had not even had the leavings from the American political table. That decision became a turning point for the Civil Rights Movement and for the Democratic Party, which for most of its history had been profoundly influenced by all-white delegations from the South (http://www.newyorktimes. com/2006/ 08/ 19/ obituaries/19adams.html).

Ida Wells Barnett, activist and writer, was born a slave in Holly Springs, Mississippi in 1862. In the 1890s she brought international attention to the lynching of African Americans in the South. At the age of 16, she became primary caregiver to her six brothers and sisters, when both of her parents died from yellow fever. After completing her studies at Rust College near Holly Springs, where her father had sat on the Board of Trustees before his death, Wells divided her time between caring for her siblings and teaching school. She moved to Memphis, Tennessee in the 1880s. Wells first began protesting the treatment of black southerners. On a train ride between Memphis and her job at a rural school, the conductor told her that she must move to the train's smoking car. Wells refused, arguing that she had purchased a first-class ticket. The conductor and other passengers then tried to physically remove her from the train. Wells returned to Memphis, hired a lawyer, and sued the Chesapeake and Ohio Railroad Company. The court decided in her favor, awarding Wells $500. The railroad company appealed, and in 1887 the Supreme Court of Tennessee reversed the decision. Using the pseudonym "Iola," Wells began to write editorials in black newspapers that challenged Jim Crow laws in the South. She bought a share of a Memphis newspaper, The Free Speech, and used it to further the cause of African American civil rights. After the lynching of three of her friends in 1892, Wells became one of the nation's most vocal anti-lynching activists. Her friends, Calvin McDowell, Thomas Moss, and Henry Stewart owned the people's grocery in Memphis, but their economic success angered the white owners of a store across the street. On March 9, a group of white men gathered to confront McDowell, Moss, and Stewart. During the ensuing scuffle, several of the white men received injuries, and authorities arrested the three black business owners. A white mob subsequently broke into the jail, captured McDowell, Moss, and Stewart, and lynched them (http:// www. blackpast.org?q=aah/barnett-ida-wells-1862-1931).

CHAPTER 15

UNRESOLVED CIVIL RIGHTS MURDERS

T HERE ARE HUNDREDS of unresolved or unprosecuted civil rights murders in the United States. In the late 1980s, the Southern Poverty Law Center conducted research on racially motivated killings that occurred between 1954 and 1968, primarily during the Civil Rights Movement. The FBI also began reviewing unresolved civil rights murders and racially motivated killings. The list included 51 victims in 39 cases. The Southern Poverty Law Center reported that there were dozens of additional victims of racial violence that were not included because there was not enough known about the circumstances of their death. It was suspected that many of these victims were killed by white supremacists to intimidate the black community or to thwart the Civil Rights Movement. The list included 74 names of civil rights deaths, mostly in the southern states.

Of the 74 killings, almost half of them (32 or 43%) occurred in Mississippi. Georgia was second with 13 (17%); Alabama third (10/13.5%); Louisiana fourth (6/8%); North Carolina (3); Tennessee (3); Arkansas (2); South Carolina (2); and Florida, Kentucky and New York with one each (Richard Cohen, Criminal Investigative Division, Southern Poverty Law Center, Correspondence to the FBI, Civil Rights Unit, February, 2007). Notably, the vast majority of the killings occurred in southern states. Five of the names could be identified as women or females. The overwhelming majority of the killers were whites and the critical years were 1964, 1965, and 1966 at the height of the Civil Rights Movement. The list is by no means definitive, as many killings were unknown, unreported, or unrecorded.

Racially Motivated Killings in Mississippi during the Modern-Civil Rights Movement

Charles Brown, Yazoo City, 1957
Jessie Brown, Winona, 1965
Silas Caston, Jackson, 1964
Vincent Dahmon, Natchez, 1966
Woodrow Wilson Daniels, Water Valley, 1966
Pheld Evans, Canton, 1964
J.E. Evaston, Long Lake, 1955
Jasper Greenwood, Vicksburg, 1964
Jimmie Lee Griffin, Sturgis, 1965
Luther Jackson, Philadelphia, 1959
Ernest Jells, Clarksdale, 1964
John Lee, Goshen Springs, 1965
Willie Henry Lee, Rankin County, 1965
George Lowe, Indianola, 1958
Sylvester Maxwell, Canton, 1963
Robert NcNair, Pelahatchie, 1965
Clinton Melton, Sumner, 1956
Booker T. Mixon, Clarksdale, 1959
Montgomery Neimiah, Cleveland, 1964
Sam O'Quinn, Centerville, 1959
Hubert Orsby, Canton, 1964
C.H. Pickett, Yazoo City, 1958
Eilliam Ray Prather, Corinth, 1959
Johnny Queen, Fayette, 1965
Donald Rasberry, Okolona, 1965
Jessie Shelby, Yazoo City, 1956
Ed Smith, State Line, 1958
Eddie James Stewart, Jackson, 1966
Isiah Taylor, Ruleville, 1964

Freddie Lee Thomas, Batesville, 1965
Saleam Triggs, Hattiesburg, 1965
Clifton Walker, Natchez, 1964

Source: Reported by Richard Cohen, Criminal Investigative Division, Southern Poverty Law Center Correspondence to the FBI, Civil Rights Unit, February, 2007.

The killing of a young black man named Clinton Melton by a white man was one of the killings included in the list of "unsolved" civil rights murders. In 1956, Elmer Kimbell, a 35-year-old white cotton gin manager killed Clinton Melton, a black gas station attendant. Kimbell claimed that he shot in self-defense, but his story sharply conflicted with the story of Lee McGarrh, the white owner of the gas station and the story of two blacks who witnessed the killing. According to the story, the owner told Melton to fill the tank, but a few minutes later, Kimbell, who had been drinking, "rebuked" Melton, saying he only wanted two dollar worth of gas. Kimbell argued with McGarrh and left, warning Melton, "I'm going to get my gun and come back and shoot you." Kimbell returned about ten minutes later and fired three shots, hitting Melton twice in the head and once in the hand. The entire shooting was witnessed by McGarrh, who was inside the store at the time. There was public outrage was particularly strong in the Glendora community where Kimbell shot Melton and where both Kimbell and Melton were both well known. The Lion's Club adopted the following statement written by a local minister:

> We consider the taking of the life of Clinton Melton an outrage against him, the people of Glendora, against the people of Mississippi, as well as the entire human family. We intend to see that the forces of justice and right prevail in the wake of this woeful evil. We humbly confess repentance for having so lived as a community that such an evil occurrence could happen here and we offer ourselves to be used in bringing to past a better realization of the justice, righteousness and peace which is the will

of God for human society (David Halberstam, *Reporter Newspaper*, April 19, 1956, p. 3).

Despite this statement from the "good people" of the Lion's Club, in the final analysis, Kimbell was acquitted of the murder of Melton. The Kimbell case demonstrates just how strong the racist culture that existed in Tallahatchie during the 1950s contributed to injustices in the criminal justice system, even in the face of hard incriminating evidence. Thus, it was practically impossible of convicting a white man for murdering a black person only a short time after the murder of Emmett Till and the acquittal of the defendants.

CHAPTER 16

THE EMMETT TILL HERITAGE TRAIL

THE EMMETT TILL Historic Intrepid Center is a part of the Emmett Till Heritage Trail, which consists of 12 sites that are dispersed over a three-county area (Tallahatchie, Leflore, and Sunflower Counties). Historical markers have been erected at many of the sites connected with the Emmett Till murder and trial. These historic markers bear testimony to the historical events surrounding the Emmet Till murder and trial that have significance for the Civil Rights Movement in America. Each year thousands of tourists visit this area to see and learn from these sites and events. Several of the major sites and historic markers of the Emmett Till Heritage Trail are included in this section.

Mississippi Valley State University

Mississippi Valley State University, established in 1950, is located in Itta Bena, Mississippi in Leflore County about 25 miles south of Glendora. Visitors to the Emmett Till Heritage Trail should visit this historic university that played a major role in providing opportunities for persons from the Delta and beyond to acquire a college education. The university has a repository of records and documents pertaining to the Emmet Till case and is home of the Delta Research and Cultural Institute (DRCI). DRCI has been instrumental in providing education about the Emmett Till case and has assisted many groups and municipalities in the development of cultural heritage tourism to promote economic development in the Delta. The Institute also provided technical assistance for the development of the Emmett Till Memorial Commission and the Emmett Till Historic Intrepid Center in Glendora. Dr. Marvin Haire, director of the Institute, conducted numerous tours for many groups to the Emmett Till Heritage Trail that contributed to both education and economic development of the area. It would be highly beneficial for visitors who come to tour the Emmett Till Heritage Trail to first stop at the Delta Research and Cultural Institute at Mississippi Valley State University in order to gain a better understanding of what they will see and experience while touring the sites along the trail.

Bryant's Grocery

Fourteen-year-old Emmett Till came to this site to buy candy in August 1955. White storekeeper Carolyn Bryant accused the black youth of flirting with her and shortly thereafter, Till was abducted by Bryant's husband and his half-brother, J.W. Milam. Till's tortured body was later found in the Tallahatchie River. The two men were tried and acquitted by an all-white male jury, but later sold their murder confession to Look Magazine for $4,000. Till's death received international attention and is widely credited with sparking the American Civil Rights Movement.

River Site Marker

This is the site where Till's body was removed from the river. It was then taken to Greenwood, Mississippi. The body was sent back to Money, Mississippi for burial. Via a phone call from Till's mother, "not to bury her son," the body was then taken back to Greenwood. The body was then sent to Tutwiler, Mississippi for final preparation to be sent to Chicago, Illinois.

The Black Bayou Bridge

According to local residents and alleged eyewitnesses, Emmett Till's body was dumped from the Black Bayou Bridge that is located near the southern end of the town. Each year many tourists visit this site to hear local residents tell stories about how and where Emmett Till was murdered that have been passed down through the generations through oral history stories. The Black Bayou runs into the Tallahatchie River just a short distance around the bend where news reports say Till's body was eventually found.

Emmett Till Murder Trial
Sumner Courthouse

In August 1955, the body of Emmett Till, a 14-yer-old black youth from Chicago, was found in the Tallahatchie River. On September 23 in a five-day trial held in this courthouse, an all-white male jury acquitted two white men, Roy Bryant and J.W. Milam, of the murder. Both later confessed to the murder in a magazine interview. The murder, coupled with the trial and acquittal of the two men, drew international attention and galvanized the Civil Rights Movement in Mississippi and the nation.

King's Place Juke Joint

This is the site where a black reporter, James Hicks, discovered information pertinent to the trial for the murder of 14-year-old Emmett Till in 1955. Here a young woman revealed to Hicks the real name of Leroy "Too Tight" Collins, as well as Henry Lee Loggins, allegedly witnesses in the Till murder, who had been incarcerated in the Charleston jail under false names and false charges. Hicks was the only reporter to go into the black community to research evidence in the Till case. Adjacent to this site was the store of J.W. Milam, one of Till's murderers.

The Delta Inn

The Delta Inn was built circa 1920 in Sumner as a railroad and residence hotel by Mr. Zachariah Edwards Jennings. The Delta

Inn was where the jury in the Bryant/Milam trial for the racially motivated murder of 14-year-old Emmett Till stayed in September 1955. During the trial, the KKK burned a cross in the front of the Inn.

Clinton Melton Marker

The September 1956 acquittal of J.W. Milam and Roy Bryant for the murder of 14-year-old Emmett Till fueled further racial violence. Clinton Melton was an outspoken black man who was gunned down here two and a half months later by Milam's friend, Elmer Kimball, allegedly over a dispute about filling up a gas tank. On the day before Kimball's trial in Sumner, Melton's widow, Beulah, was apparently forced off the road near Glendora and drowned in Black Bayou, leaving five children orphaned. Kimball was acquitted of Clinton's murder.

Emmett Till Memorial Park and Interpretive Nature Trail

The Emmett Till Memorial Park and Interpretive Nature Trail was one of the components of the community revitalization plan to promote cultural heritage tourism. The plan also included the Emmett Till Museum, the Sonny Boy Williams II Museum and Hall of Fame, and the Sonny Boy Williamson II Blues Café. Ironically, the park is located on the southwest end of the town near the Black Bayou, where the body of Emmett Till was disposed before he was brutally murdered. The park serves as a memorial in honor of Emmett Till in hope that it would help attract tourists who want to learn the story of Emmett Till from the local residents who live in the area, as well as the culture of the people who live in the town of Glendora. The Emmett Till Memorial Park was designed to accommodate cultural tourism events such as fairs, blues festivals, concerts, picnics, and cultural events and to provide a place for community events for local residents. One of the annual events held in the park is the Sonny Boy Williamson II Blues and Heritage Festival. The park was dedicated on September 10, 2008.

Getting To Glendora

Visitors to Glendora coming from the north may come either via Interstate 55 South to Highway 82 West, to Greenwood, then Highway 49 north to Glendora. Alternatively, visitors may take the scenic route through the Delta via Highway 49 South to Clarksdale and on to Glendora. Visitors from the South may come via Interstate 55 North to Highway 82 West to Greenwood, and north on Highway 49 to Glendora. Visitors from the east or west may travel via Interstate 20 to Jackson, Mississippi, take Interstate 55 north, and then follow the same route. Highway 49 has been designated as the Emmett Till Memorial Highway. Private automobiles or tour buses are the preferred ways to get to Glendora.

If you rewind the clock to 1952, in order to get to Glendora you would have to travel on a dirt road. If you were fortunate, you could come by automobile, but you could also get there by bus, wagon, horseback, or perhaps a boat ride up the Tallahatchie River. On a recent excursion to Glendora, we traveled through Greenwood, the capital of the "cotton kingdom" during the heyday when cotton was "king" in the 1850s, up to around 1950. Traveling west on highway 82, just west of the town limits of Greenwood, we made a right turn onto Highway 49. This junction was once a famous place where northbound travelers went to catch a ride to stations as far as Memphis and Chicago. Highway 49 was one of the major arteries of the Blues Highway that was a common route in the Delta travelled by blues singers during the days when blues was king.

Epilogue

W E WROTE THIS book to tell our story of the trials, tribulations, and triumphs of the town of Glendora and its struggle to rise above historical conditions that were created by slavery, Jim Crow, poverty, and the brutal murder of a 14-year-old boy named Emmett Till that energized the Civil Rights Movement in America. Glendora is the place where Johnny B. Thomas rose from the son of sharecroppers to Mayor, who has led his community for the past 35 years. During this period, he has worked diligently to transform his town from a "mountain of despair" into a "stone of hope" that Dr. Martin Luther King, Jr. envisioned in his "I Have A Dream" speech in Washington, D.C. in August 1963. All of these events are part of the heritage of Glendora, a small rural town located in the heart of the Mississippi Delta.

While the history of Glendora cannot be changed, we can use our history to inspire the people to change the adverse conditions that have plagued this community for many decades. We resolve to never let the negative history, whether created by us or forced upon us, repeat itself. We will continue to fight for civil rights and against civil injustices in all forms, including racial inequality in the distribution of wealth, power, and privilege that are still all too common. We will also continue to fight against poverty, family dissolution, imprisonment of our youth, and racial discrimination and inequality in employment, education, and political participation. We will not be defeated by the evils of the past or let the sins of our father determine our future.

In 2005, forty-two years after the "Dream" Glendora opened a memorial museum in honor of Emmett Till as part of a community cultural heritage tourism project to promote community economic development and revitalization. The crown jewel of the cultural heritage tourism project was the Emmett Till Historic Intrepid Center that included the tragic murder of Emmett Till and the history and culture of the people of Glendora and Tallahatchie County. The people of Glendora were optimistic that the project would be successful and had great hope that it would provide the stimulus to turn Glendora's past mountain of despair into a thriving stone of hope. Although the Emmett Till Museum has only been opened for a few years, it has played a major role in preserving the history and culture of Glendora and Tallahatchie County, serving as a source of education for visitors and tourists, and generating revenue for the town. However, the years ahead will determine if our dream and hope for economic prosperity can be sustained.

As another chapter in the history of Glendora comes to a close, we extend our sincere thanks to the matriarchs and patriarchs of Glendora and Tallahatchie County, who have overcome their own "mountains of despair" through their great faith and works. In looking to the future, we pledge to make the necessary investment in our youth to ensure a brighter future for their community, with the realization that there can be no strong community without strong families and youth. We must leave no youth behind! We have endeavored to prepare a cadre of young leaders to take our place and carry our community to even greater heights. In a real sense, the youth of Glendora are our new stone of hope!